EDITOR: MARTIN W

OSPREY
MILITARY

MEN-AT-ARM

THE ARM
GUSTAVUS ADOLPHUS
1 INFANTRY

Text by
RICHARD BRZEZINSKI
Colour plates by
RICHARD HOOK *and*
RICHARD BRZEZINSKI

Published in 1991 by
Osprey Publishing Ltd
59 Grosvenor Street, London W1X 9DA
© Copyright 1991 Osprey Publishing Ltd

British Library Cataloguing in Publication Data
Brzezinski, Richard
  Gustavus Adolphus's army.
  I
  1. Sweden. Armies, history
  I. Title   II. Series
  356.09485

  ISBN 0-85045-997-4

Filmset in Great Britain
Printed through Bookbuilders Ltd, Hong Kong

Dedication
For Ingetora

Author's note
This is the first of two books dealing with the
equipment, uniforms and organisation of the Swedish
army. This volume describes mainly the infantry; the
second will cover cavalry, artillery and tactics, and will
include a bibliography and acknowledgements. The
timespan extends slightly beyond Gustavus
Adolphus's lifetime (1594–1632) to cover the whole of
the so-called 'Swedish phase' (1630–35) of the Thirty
Years' War. There has unfortunately been no room to
examine the important part played by the Swedes in
the later years of the Thirty Years' War of 1618–48.

   This study is based mostly on untranslated Swedish
works and on contemporary memoirs and journals. It
also includes much previously unpublished material
from Swedish and German archives. Michael
Roberts's *Gustavus Adolphus* (2 vols.; Edinburgh,
1953–58) has been a useful starting point, and is still
the most detailed modern source available in English
for the historical background.

Currency, date and measurement conventions
Money is quoted in Riksdaler (Rdr.)—a Swedish
corruption of Reichsthaler, the Imperial German
currency—which was the closest thing to a standard
Euro-currency in its day. In the 1620s/30s the
exchange rate was roughly 4.5 Rdr. = £1 sterling.

   From 1582 two calendars existed side-by-side in
Christian Europe. In line with current convention,
dates for events in Sweden are left in the 'Old Style'
calendar and with the year beginning on 1 January.
Those in Continental Europe are in the 'New Style'.
To convert dates from Old Style to New add 10 days:
so that 6 May (O.S.) becomes 16 May (N.S.).

   From 1605, the Swedish 'Rydaholm' ell was the
standard unit of length; it equalled 0.5934 metres or
1ft. $11\frac{1}{3}$ in.

INTRODUCTION

'Consider the great Gustavus Adolphus! In eighteen months he won one battle, lost a second, and was killed in a third. His fame was won at bargain price!' (Napoleon to Gaspar Gourgaud, 1818)

The rapid rise to fame of Gustavus Adolphus was indeed extraordinary. For a time he had the status of figures like Alexander the Great and Napoleon: men who have inspired their armies to perform incredible feats; men almost worshipped in their own lifetimes.

His grip on the popular imagination in his day was based at least partly on something far more mysterious than his wide-ranging abilities. A prophecy of 1549 made by Paracelsus, a contemporary of Nostradamus, had foretold a series of worldwide disasters that would only end when a Golden Lion came from the north to defeat the Eagle.

The disasters seemed to begin in 1618, when the Thirty Years' War broke out, and the Catholic Emperor of Germany, whose emblem was the black eagle, went on the rampage in Protestant Germany. In 1630 Gustavus—the last champion of the Protestants—came to the rescue. His landings in north Germany were accompanied by reports of battles in the clouds and bizarre deformed births. On his steady march south he smashed the Catholics at Breitenfeld in central Germany. In 1632 he entered Augsburg, the birthplace of Lutheran Protestantism, and was received as the 'Lion of the North'; few doubted that in the following year he would march on the Eagle's nest in Vienna. Unfortunately, in November 1632 Gustavus (by this time looking, perhaps, to his own predicted destiny) was killed in an imprudent cavalry charge at the battle of Lützen.

The Age of Reason has replaced the 'Lion of the North' myth with another that surrounds him with an aura almost as mystical. It has turned him into a superhuman genius responsible for all manner of things: technical innovations (the military uniform,

The 'Lion of the North': Gustavus Adolphus (Gustav II Adolf), King of Sweden. There can be no doubt that he was exceptional; tall and blond, educated and culture-loving, with the conviction of an evangelist and the bluntness of a sergeant-major, he made a lasting impression on all who met him. Already in this 1632 print with the incredible victory at Breitenfeld behind him, a hint of superiority and impatience with his German allies had appeared on his face. (Print by Matthaeus Merian of Frankfurt)

leather cannon, the 'Swedish feather', paper bullet cartridges, abolition of the musket rest); administrative reforms (conscript standing armies, the infantry brigade, military logistics, huge increases in the size of armies, standardisation of artillery calibres); and tactical innovations (dashing cavalry charges, offensive infantry formations, volley fire, close artillery support from regimental pieces).

1594 9 Dec.: Gustavus Adolphus born.

1611 He inherits throne; crowned Oct. 1617.

1611–13 'Kalmar War'. Danes invade Sweden and take Kalmar (May 1611) and Sweden's chief North Sea port, Älvsborg (May 1612). Swedes must pay a million Rdr. ransom for Älvsborg.

1611–17 *War with Russia*. De La Gardie takes Novgorod (1611). Gustavus's brother Karl Filip is almost elected Tzar (1613). Gustavus besieges Pskov (1615). Peace of Stolbova (1617).

1620 Gustavus visits Germany to marry Maria Eleanora of Brandenburg.

1621–26 Conquest of Livonia (Latvia):

1621–22 1st campaign: Gustavus captures the capital *Riga* (25 Sept.) in a few weeks, a feat his father had been attempting for 11 years.

1623–24 Sweden prepares for Polish invasion.

1625–26 2nd campaign: Latvia captured as far as Dvina River. At *Wallhof* (Walmojza) (17 Jan. 1626) Gustavus defeats Poles in his first open field battle.

1626–29 Conquest of Polish Prussia:

1626 6 July: Gustavus lands at Pillau, quickly takes Elbing, Marienberg and seizes control of the Vistula. 22 Sept.–1 Oct.: *Battles at Mewe (Gniew)*. Polish cavalry halted by musket fire.

1627 16 April: *Battle of Hammerstein (Czarne)*; 2,500 German mercenaries surrender to the Poles. 18 May: Fresh army lands and marches on Danzig, but Gustavus is wounded (2/3 June) crossing Vistula. 7/8 Aug.: *Battle of Dirschau (Tczew)*: Almost a major victory, but Gustavus shot in the neck. 28 Nov.: *Naval battle at Oliva*.

1628 Small scale campaigning, hampered by devastation of Prussia and plague. June: *Swedes relieve Stralsund* which is under siege by the Imperialists under Wallenstein.

1629 12 Feb.: *Battle of Górzno*. Herman Wrangel defeats Poles. 26 June: *Cavalry battle at Stuhm/Honigfelde (Trzciana)*. Poles with Imperialist help defeat Gustavus. 26 Sept.: Poles and Swedes agree to six-year Truce of Altmark.

1630–35 'Swedish Phase' of the Thirty Years' War. Gustavus comes to rescue of the German Protestants.

1630 The bridgehead in *North Germany*. He lands at Peenemünde (16 July), captures Stettin and gradually evicts Imperialists from Pomerania.

1631 Advance into *central Germany*. 13 April: Frankfurt-an-der-Oder stormed. 20 May: *Sack of Magdeburg* by the Catholics: 30,000 die. 22 June: Brandenburg makes alliance with Sweden. 27 July: Devastating night attack on Catholic cavalry at *Burgstall*. Sept.: Saxony, Bremen, and Hesse-Kassel ally themselves with Sweden. 17 Sept.: *Battle of Breitenfeld ('Leipzig')*. Swedes/Saxons defeat Tilly's Catholic League veterans. Sept.–Nov.: Swedes occupy Germany north of line from Mannheim to Prague. Winter: Gustavus sets up his 'General-Government' of Germany at Frankfurt-am-Main.

1632 Into Catholic *south Germany*. April: *Battle of Rain ('Crossing of the Lech')*. Catholics defeated, Tilly killed. Augsburg and Munich captured. 3 Sept.: *Storm of Alte Feste*, Nuremberg— Gustavus defeated while assaulting Wallenstein's camp. 16 Nov.: *Battle of Lützen*. Gustavus killed. Swedes are too stunned to follow up Imperialists.

1633–35 *Sweden defensive*: Oxenstierna takes over rule for Gustavus's young daughter Christina.

1633 23 April: *Heilbronn League* formed to control Swedish/Protestant forces in Germany. Army mutinies. 8 July: *Battle of Oldendorf*. Swedish/Protestant victory. October: *Battle of Steinau*. Wallenstein captures a Swedish army and reconquers Silesia.

1634 25 Feb.: Wallenstein assassinated. 22 April: Brandenburg breaks off alliance with Sweden. 6 Sept.: *Battle of Nördlingen*. Spanish/Imperialists destroy main Swedish/Protestant army. South and central Germany fall.

1635 30 May: *Peace of Prague*. Saxony breaks with Sweden and joins Emperor. August: army mutinies—Oxenstierna held hostage. 12 Sept.: *Peace of Stuhmsdorf*. Prussian conquests returned to Poland, but Livonia becomes officially Swedish. April, Oct.: *French-Swedish alliances*. Best mercenaries go with Bernhard of Weimar to French service. '*French phase*' of Thirty Years' *War* begins.

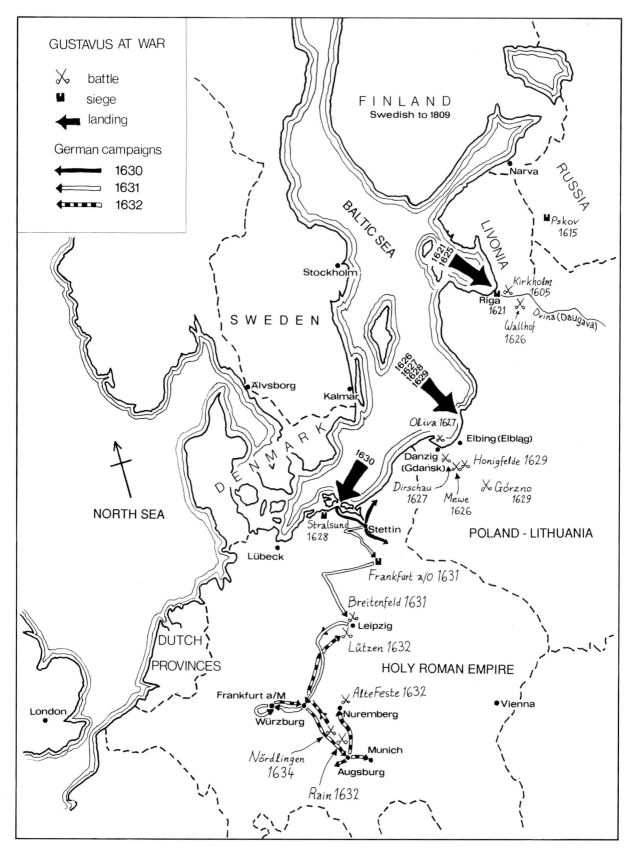

GUSTAVUS AT WAR

⚔ battle

🏰 siege

⬅ landing

German campaigns
⬅ 1630
⬅ 1631
⬅ 1632

FINLAND
Swedish to 1809

BALTIC SEA

RUSSIA

Narva

LIVONIA

Pskov
1615

Stockholm

1621
1625

Kirkholm
1605

SWEDEN

Riga
1621

Dvina (Daugava)

Wallhof
1626

Älvsborg

Kalmar

1626
1627
1628
1629

Oliva 1627

Elbing (Elbląg)

Danzig
(Gdańsk)

Honigfelde 1629

NORTH SEA

DENMARK

1630

Dirschau
1627

Mewe
1626

Górzno
1629

POLAND - LITHUANIA

Stralsund
1628

Stettin

Lübeck

Frankfurt a/0 1631

DUTCH

PROVINCES

Breitenfeld 1631

Leipzig

Lützen 1632

HOLY ROMAN EMPIRE

Frankfurt a/M

AlteFeste 1632

Nuremberg

Vienna

London

Würzburg

Munich

Nördlingen
1634

Augsburg

Rain 1632

5

The greatest of 19th and early 20th-century military historians have even gone so far as to call him 'the father of modern armies', and the inventor of 'total war'. Of course, no one single man could ever have achieved all these innovations. The problem is, what exactly did he do?

The Swedish background

Sweden began the 17th century as an insignificant backwater, where many southern Europeans believed only wild savages lived. If it was not for the trading power of the Hanseatic League, Sweden might have slept through the Renaissance entirely. Thanks to the Hansa, though, Sweden made strong links with the German port of Lübeck; and in return for her copper, Sweden took on a thin veneer of German culture.

Since 1397, the three ancient Scandinavian kingdoms—Sweden, Denmark and Norway—had been subject to Danish rule. (Finland until 1809 was part of Sweden.) In 1523 the Swedes broke away and elected Gustav Vasa as their king. Gustav founded the great Vasa dynasty. He had three sons: Erik XIV who ruled after him (1560–68), Johan III (ruled 1568–92), and Duke Karl.

In 1592 Johan III's son Sigismund succeeded him on the throne. Sigismund had been brought up as a Catholic by his Polish mother, and in 1587 had been elected king of Poland. His staunch Catholic views soon led to conflict, and he was deposed by Gustav Vasa's third son Duke Karl in 1599. In 1607 Duke Karl was crowned as Karl IX. However, Sigismund returned to his Polish kingdom determined to recover his Swedish crown. So began the feuding and subsequent devastating wars between Polish and Swedish Vasas which were to last until 1660 and to end in the Baltic becoming a Swedish lake.

In 1611 Karl IX died, leaving the country to his 16-year-old son, Gustavus Adolphus (the Latinised form of his Swedish name, Gustav Adolf). As well as inheriting the Polish war, Gustavus found himself with his main army absent in Russia, and with a Danish army of reconquest advancing deep into Sweden. Sweden was already in a terrible condition after decades of conflict; the state coffers were nearly empty, and the population on the verge of rebellion; the task before him was huge. The appalling state of his army must have looked like one of his lesser problems.

THE MILITARY BACKGROUND

'The Swedish cavalry in general is badly equipped, having no armour; the foot is badly clothed and armed, in fact not having a single pike in use or in possession and being mere farmers...' This was Johann of Nassau's opinion of the Swedish army in 1601. Its failings were admirably confirmed when it was virtually annihilated at Kirkholm in Latvia in 1605 by a Polish–Lithuanian force only one-third its size.

Karl IX had already tried to reform the army along the new Dutch lines. In 1601 he appointed Johann of Nassau his general-in-command of the army in Latvia, but Johann's stay was too short for the Dutch

The blood-stained shirt Gustavus wore when shot in the neck by a Polish marksman at Dirschau in 1627. He never wore metal armour again because of the resulting soreness in his shoulder, and he found it difficult to use his right arm. The three shirts he was wearing when killed at Lützen also survive, but have been even more heavily mutilated than this shirt to provide relics for visiting dignitaries. (Livrustkammaren—hereafter, LRK)

system that he attempted to introduce to take a lasting hold. Little of the Dutch system had been written down when Gustavus began his schooling. The bulk of his early reading consisted of the conventional military textbooks—describing the Spanish–German or 'Landsknecht' system then in use in Sweden.

In 1608 Karl called in Jakob de la Gardie, who had just returned from Dutch service, to give Gustavus two months of tuition in Dutch techniques. The Chancellor commented that during this short period the 13-year-old Gustavus began to talk 'almost incessantly about other peoples' wars, battles, sieges, the art of war on land and water, shipping and sea-travel'.

By 1610, the young Gustavus was already dabbling in matters of military importance and had asked for a military command. When Denmark invaded Sweden in 1611 his impatience could no longer be contained, and he joined the army in the front line. In 1614 he was setting off for Narva on the Russian border for his first campaign overseas; and in 1615 he took control of the (unsuccessful) siege of Pskov in Russia.

With the Russian war finally ended in 1617, and the question of his rights to the crown settled by his coronation in October 1617, Gustavus was able to turn to the reform of his army. Immediately he made use of his links with Holland. The Dutch, since 1613, had been buying immense consignments of copper to help Sweden pay off the 1 million Rdr. 'Älvsborg ransom' to Denmark. From 1617 Gustavus sent some of his veterans of Dutch service—Nils Stiernsköld, Antoni Monier and James Seton—shuttling between Sweden and Holland. They asked for mercenaries, arms and armour, and technical assistance with his artillery. Much of this was paid for with Swedish copper.

Meanwhile, important events were taking place in Germany: the Thirty Years' War was brewing, and the German towns were becoming increasingly uneasy. A movement called *Landesdefension* (Defence of the Land) had developed to help the small German states to protect themselves with locally recruited militias. It took the best of the new Dutch ideas and refined them for a German market. The chief minds at work were Johann of Nassau, and Johann Jacob von Wallhausen, author of influential military manuals for infantry—*L'Art Militaire pour l'infanterie* (1615); cavalry—*Kriegskunst zu Pferd*

Johann, Count of Nassau-Siegen (1561–1623), who along with his cousin Prince Maurits, Stadholder of the United Dutch Provinces, and his brother Willem Lodewijk of Nassau, was at the heart of the Dutch reforms. Relearning the lost skills of Classical armies from translations of Roman military manuals, they reorganised battle formations to make them more flexible and to increase firepower. Johann was the brains behind the most famous of all drill manuals, de Gheyn's Wapenhandelinghe… (Exercise of Armes) of 1607; and the founder of one of the first military academies, at Siegen in Germany. His importance in the spread of Dutch ideas to Protestant Germany and Sweden is only slowly coming to be appreciated. (Museum des Siegerlandes, Siegen)

(1616); and artillery—*Archiley–Kriegskunst* (1617). Johann of Nassau made Wallhausen director of the new military academy at Siegen in Germany which he opened in 1616. *Landesdefension* was exactly what Gustavus was looking for: it was based on locally raised troops, and was cheap.

Gustavus's visit to Germany, 1620–21

In 1620 Gustavus visited Germany ostensibly to get married. He spent a good deal of time roaming

six deep. In July 1621 he published his Articles of War, determined to stamp out 'the insignificant military discipline and order that have hitherto been tolerated…'.

Also in 1621, Wallhausen published *Defensio Patriae oder Landrettung*, an instruction book on how to put together a German militia army in the Dutch manner. His recommendations bear more than passing similarity to Gustavus's chief reforms:

'Companies of 150 men… are strong enough… the more officers they have the better they are.' As for *rots* (files), 'the best convenience will you have if you make them 6 strong,… then you can march them six strong in the open field, and in half rots, three strong on narrow roads' (an important consideration on Sweden's constricted tracks). Wallhausen also detailed a huge variety of other minutiae, ranging from the best types of clothing, down to the colour of tilts for the army's wagons.

It is often said that Gustavus was personally responsible for turning Dutch military theories into a workable military system. This is not entirely correct: what he adopted between 1617 and 1622, was, with a few changes, basically a refined Protestant German version of the Dutch system.

The title page of Troupitz's Kriegs Kunst nach Königlicher Schwedischer Manier… *(Art of War in the Royal Swedish Manner). Printed in 1638 (though completed by 1633), it was the first manual describing Swedish drill in any detail. It borrowed heavily from Wallhausen's influential manuals—even this title page is little more than a reworking of Wallhausen's 1615 infantry manual, though the musketeer and pikeman have been redrawn in 1630s clothing. (Uppsala University Library—hereafter, UUB)*

THE CONSCRIPT ARMY

around German princedoms disguised as 'Captain Gars' (an acronym formed from his title Gustavus Adolphus Rex Sueciae). On 28 May (O.S.) he visited Johann of Nassau in Heidelberg. The events of the day were recorded in the diary of a fellow traveller: '…we followed Count Johann of Nassau into his chambers. There he showed us with little papers how he would deploy an army in battle, in what way he thinks a regular fortress should be built. And then took us into the arsenal, there we saw two types of wagons fitted with pikes and small iron-guns (*skrotstycker*)…'.

Gustavus returned to Sweden and within two years had introduced his most important reforms. He reduced his infantry companies from 272 men to 150, and his infantry formations from eight or ten ranks to

If one of Gustavus's achievements has been singled out by historians as his greatest, it is probably the creation of a permanent conscript army—one of the first in Europe to be organised into regiments with regional affiliations. Even here, the credit should not all go to Gustavus. His uncle, Erik XIV, had already achieved something similar in the 1560s with his (admittedly short-lived) national 'great-regiments', and even these were merely an extension of a medieval militia system, of a type that had largely died out elsewhere in Europe.

Conscription

Utskrivning or conscription, as a means of raising infantry in Sweden, also dates back to the mid-16th century—the cavalry were mostly volunteers.

Thanks to poor administration and widespread corruption, conscription was not working well until Gustavus laid down firm guidelines and began to enforce them strictly.

His regulations of 1620 made all males over 15 years old liable for conscription. When an *utskrivning* was ordered, the men of a district were divided up into files (*rotar*) of ten men, and each file was lined up before army commissioners in the local meeting hall. One man was selected from the ten, usually a robust peasant of 18 to 40 years of age, but preferably young. His clothing and sword were paid for, in theory at least, from the 'file-money' (*Rote-penningar*) contributed by the nine remaining men of his file. He was then taken to the locally based regiment and trained rigorously before setting off on campaign.

The Provincial Regiments

The success of the system—foreigners marvelled at how mere farmers' lads could be turned into disciplined soldiers—relied on the establishment of permanent provincial regiments. These went through three distinct phases of development: the peacetime *Landsregiment* (1617); the peacetime *Landsregiment* composed for war of three Field-Regiments (c.1625); and finally, the Provincial Regiment (c.1630).

The first stage was set up in 1617 by Chancellor Axel Oxenstierna rather than Gustavus. He divided the kingdom into eight military districts, each of which was to supply a *Landsregiment*: two in Finland, the other six in Sweden (Norrland, Uppland, Södermanland, Östergötland, Västergötland, and Små-

land). Each *Landsregiment* was commanded by a 'land colonel'; and was made up, in theory, of 3,600 men, organised in six administrative 'squadrons' (not to be confused with tactical squadrons). However, the *Landsregiments* were peacetime administrative units only. Prior to a campaign men were drafted out and reorganised into separate regiments for use in the field.

By the end of 1625 it was seen that these 'field-regiments' should have a permanent existence. As a result the *Landsregiment* began to consist of three field-regiments (*Fältregiment*). Either one or two were sent abroad, the remainder staying at home to defend the province from invasion.

With war becoming the normal state of affairs in the late 1620s, it was realised that a separate peacetime organisation was unnecessary: the field-

A company drawn up for training in the Swedish manner, from Troupitz's manual. The central block is made up of pikemen and the two wings are of musketeers; each block has its own drummer. The company's three commissioned officers—captain, ensign (with flag), and lieutenant—lead the blocks. The two sergeants (responsible for drill and battle order) watch the sides; and three 'under-officers'—Furier, Führer-of-colours (ensign's assistant), and Rüstmeister (captain-of-

arms)—bring up the rear. The fourth 'under-officer', the muster clerk, did not normally fight in the field.

The illustration is, however, incorrect in several crucial details. The pike block should have nine files under three corporals; the musketeers should have only twelve files under three corporals in all. Troupitz probably illustrates a late German variant, which compensates for the increasing shortage of pikemen in the 1630s. The artillery pieces are purely decorative.

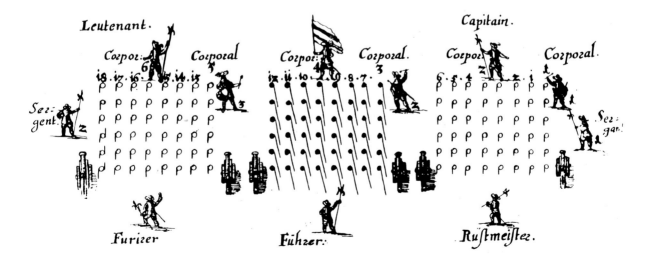

regiments were the most practical units both in war and peacetime. The *Landsregiment* was abandoned and its territory distributed among the field-regiments. Each of these developed into a provincial-regiment (*Landskapsregiment*).

Gustavus's reforms were finally set in concrete by the 1634 government constitution—effectively a charter for the army. The document included a list of the provincial-regiments in order of precedence. When regimental numbering was introduced it followed this ranking system, and remained essentially unchanged until 1925.

The provincial-regiments of 1634 (most of which were already in existence by 1630) were as follows:

Sweden		*Finland*
Uppland	Älvsborg	Åbo-län
Skaraborg	Västergötland-	Björneborg
Södermanland	Dalsland	Tavastehus
Kronoberg	Västmanland	Viborg
Jönköping	Västerbotten	Savolax
Dalarna	Kalmar	Nyland
(Dal-regt.)	Närke-Värmland	Österbotten
Östergötland		
Halsinge		

The human cost

Between 1626 and 1630 an average of 10,000 men were conscripted each year, with a peak in 1627 of 13,500. This amounted to 2% of the entire male population each year. As the drainage of manpower increased in the 1630s, boys of 15–17 began to be conscripted.

In some northern areas of Sweden the effects were disastrous. A now notorious study by J. Lindegren has revealed the effects on the parish of Bygdeå, which in 1620 consisted of about 250 farmsteads with 1,900 people in all. By 1639 the population had fallen to about 1,700. The male population between 15 and 60 had dropped even more dramatically, from 468 in 1621 to only 288 in 1639. Of 230 men conscripted, only 15 ever returned alive.

The study also reveals that the mortality rate among Bygdeå conscripts in Prussia and Pomerania averaged 50% per year, almost all from illness rather than enemy action. The worst years by far were 1627 to 1629 when Gustavus was bogged down in Polish Prussia. Conscription to the Swedish infantry, in effect, amounted to a death sentence.

Each Rot (file) contains 6 'Marching men':
1 Corporal (C) or Rotmaster (R)
4 Common soldiers
1 Under-rotmaster (file-closer)

The basic building block of Gustavus's infantry was the regiment (not the brigade, as sometimes suggested). Its size was fixed by Gustavus in 1621 at eight companies each nominally of 150 men. A few larger regiments of 12 and 16 companies also began to appear from 1628. Regiments with other numbers of companies had usually failed to reach strength.

The regimental staff seems to have varied somewhat at the colonel's discretion, but the company staff was fixed at 16 men—a very high number for armies of the time, which gave the Swedes advantages in initiative and flexibility, and allowed the company to function as a separate body in small or remote garrisons. 'Muster-boys' were officer's servants: two were allowed to the captain and one each for lieutenant and ensign. 'Passevolants' were non-existent men whose salary compensated the captain for replacing deserters and men who died of illness; the state was only responsible for making up losses due to enemy action. In practice, the allowance seems to have been reduced from 14 men to 10% of company effectives.

Though the establishment strength of an eight-company regiment was officially 1,200 men, in practice it numbered only 128 officers (excluding regimental staff) and 1,008 'marching men' (432 pikemen and 576 musketeers). The 150 man company, in fact, numbered only 16 officers and 126 men (54 pikemen and 72 musketeers).

MERCENARIES

There was a limit to the burden Gustavus could place on his own citizens. Already in the early 1620s he had widespread rioting on his hands. His only option was to increase the number of foreign mercenaries.

The word 'mercenaries' has unfortunate connotations today, and modern Swedes prefer to call them 'enlisted' (*värvade*) troops, the term actually used by Gustavus's administration to distinguish them from conscripted troops. They were mostly volunteers raised by a recruiting party attracting men to the regiment by the beat of a drum. Nevertheless they were normally foreigners, usually Germans, for whom the main attraction of the Swedish army was seldom more complicated than adventure and, of course, money.

The mercenary system relied entirely on a few enterprising officers who had access to large sums of money. The chief of a regiment was normally a colonel, who received a personal patent from Gustavus to raise a regiment, which thereafter was virtually his own private property. As well as earning a substantial salary, such a colonel-proprietor treated his regiment as a profit-making business. The worst colonels fleeced their soldiers mercilessly for every *Riksdaler* they were worth, and, in the words of one Scots officer, often 'could only be induced to pay when they had exhausted every means of evasion'.

One of the reasons that foreigners flocked to Gustavus's ranks was the prospect of rapid promotion, and the smell of money that this entailed. A good example is Christof von Houwald (or Hubald). Born in 1602 the son of a Saxon clothmaker, he joined up as a common musketeer in 1616–18, and served the Emperor, Saxony, Mansfeld and Brunswick before going to Sweden in 1624. He rose steadily in the Blue Regiment: lieutenant 1625, captain 1627, major 1629, lieutenant-colonel 1630, and was made a Swedish nobleman in May 1630. In winter 1631/32, as reward for capturing an enemy fortress on his own initiative, he was commissioned as colonel of a new foot and a new horse regiment. When his regiments were disbanded after the battle of Nördlingen in 1634 he left for Saxon service as a major-general. From 1635 to 1654 he was in Poland, becoming '*overkom-*

This picture, painted in 1618, tells the extraordinary story of a group of seal-hunters from the island of Gotland who were marooned on an iceberg in 1603. They survived for 14 days until the iceberg was blown ashore. Their thick lined jackets and breeches and eastern-style fur caps should give an idea of the cold-weather dress of native Swedish infantry. (Fårö Church, Gotland)

mendant' of Danzig's garrison, and battling against Khmelnitsky's Cossack rebels at Beresteczko in 1651. He finally died in retirement on a large estate in 1663.

Though Houwald's promotion from the ranks was not typical, it was considerably more common in the Swedish army than in others. His wide international experience was not at all unusual. Before 1631, however, Gustavus rarely gave regiments to adventurers unless they came with impeccable references from other Protestant armies. He preferred, as in Houwald's case, to train his officers in his own mercenary 'coloured regiments'.

The Coloured Regiments[1]

Regiments with colour names were fashionable chiefly in Protestant states. In 1620/21 Count Mansfeld had raised Red, Blue, Yellow and Green mercenary regiments for the German Protestants; and in 1625/26 the Danes had levied a similar selection.

Sweden's first coloured regiments acquired their colour names between 1625 and 1627. Significantly,

---

[1] Not to be confused with 'coloured brigades', which were temporary groupings of regiments for campaign and battlefield use.

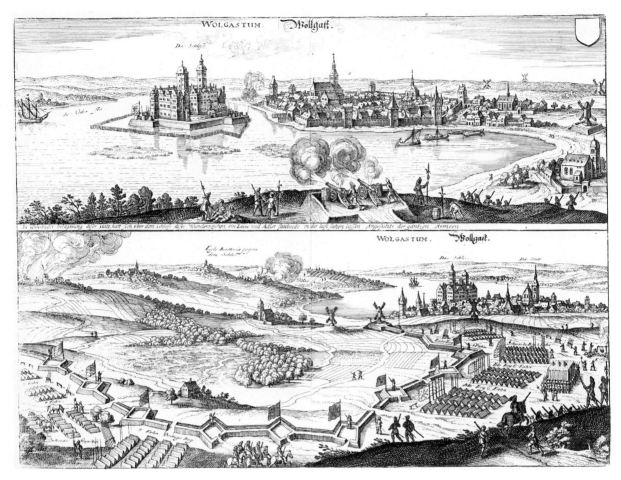

WOLGASTUM. Wolgaſt.

WOLGASTUM. Wolgaſt.

they had the same names as Mansfeld's original regiments; in fact, many of the troops had earlier served Mansfeld, and then the Danes, before coming over to Sweden. The colour names referred chiefly to flag colours (see Plate D).

The Yellow Regiment: The senior mercenary regiment, which at times was called the Court Regiment (*Hovregiment*) or Guards Regiment. It had several short-lived predecessors: 1613, the Liferegt.; 1615–16, His Majesty's Regt.; 1618–21, the Drabant Regt.; 1621–24, the (old) Hovregt. The (new) Hov-

regt. was formed in 1624, mostly from Germans; it was first called the 'Yellow Regiment' in 1626, and kept this name until it passed into French pay in 1635.

The Blue Regiment: The longest-lived mercenary regiment. It became officially known, from 1634 at the latest, as the 'Old Blue'.

The Red Regiment: The least well-known of the four—it remained in Prussia until 1631, so did not take part in the first year's campaigning in Germany.

The Green Regiment: The junior of the four, the Green Regiment has acquired a mythology all of its own, mostly because one of its colonels, John Hepburn, was a Scot. The Green Regiment was once thought to be the ancestor of the senior British regiment of the line, The Royal Scots, which in fact descended from a Scots regiment raised by Hepburn for France in 1633. Some have even speculated that the 'green' part of the regiment's name came from the green of the Scots tartan worn in the ranks. In fact,

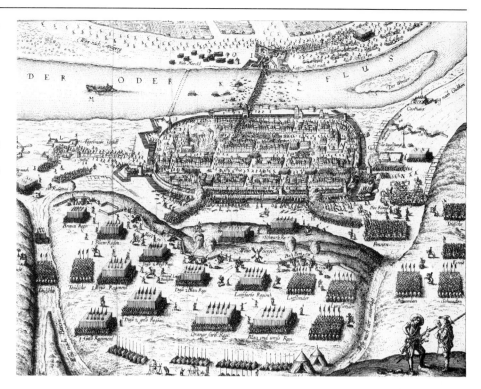

Storming of Frankfurt-an-der-Oder, April 1631. This is one of the last prints to record colour names for most infantry regiments (probably because their flags were becoming unrecognisable). The regiments are deployed in squadron-type formations (i.e. battalions) rather than brigades; the larger (12 company) regiments (Blue, Yellow and White) field two squadrons. Note also the assault columns attacking with musketeers in support. Contemporary version of a 1631 print originally by Peter Rollos. (Rijksmuseum, Amsterdam)

aside from a handful of Scots officers, there was hardly a Scot in the regiment at all. The muster rolls, which survive in the Stockholm Krigsarkivet, show mostly Germans who, in fact, were mainly Prussians recruited as part of the feudal obligations of the Duke of Brandenburg to Poland. The regiment was marching to join the Poles in July 1627 when it was intercepted by the Swedes. Israel Hoppe records the incident in his chronicle of the Prussian campaign:

'Count von Thurn shouted out: "Friends or Enemies?". To which the [Prussian] infantry replied: "Friends!". He continued: "Then shoulder your muskets!". And when this was done, he rode up and said: "Are you the King of Sweden's men?". "Ja, ja!" they answered.'

Gustavus incorporated the regiment into his army, but sent the officers back to the Duke of Brandenburg to tell him 'to take more care of his men in future'.

The New Coloured Regiments

Between 1629 and 1630, Gustavus greatly expanded his mercenary force in preparation for his landing in Germany. The four existing colour regiments were increased in size from eight companies to 12 (the Yellow and Blue Regiments later even reached 16). Many new regiments were also levied; the colonels of

some of these regiments (hoping, no doubt, to break into a select circle) adopted their own colour names:

The Black Regiments were closely related: three were raised in 1629 from German Hansa towns (mostly Emden) by *Hovmarshal* Falkenberg, and according to the contemporary historian Chemnitz (I, p.26) all were black regiments. A possible fourth black regiment was raised in early 1630 by Knyphausen, also mostly in Emden, and in Hamburg. This is probably the 'black regiment' indicated on a print of the siege of Wolgast. Interestingly, Knyphausen had been Falkenberg's Lieutenant-General in 1629.

The Orange Regiment and Brown Regiment were both raised in Prussia in early 1630 from mercenaries discharged from Polish, Brandenburg and Danzig service. Hoppe records Johann Vitzthum von Eckstädt's 'orange-coloured German regiment' twice, and Dargitz's brown regiment once.

The White Regiment was established from the garrison of Stettin which surrendered without fighting a few days after Gustavus landed in Germany.

The colour names of the new coloured regiments, unlike the old ones, were not normally used in official correspondence. Initially, they were all intended to have 12 companies, but quickly all but the White Regiment were reduced to eight. Note that there were many more mercenary units without colour names, and these were known instead after the name of their colonel.

Table A: Mercenary Regiments with Colour Names

The four old coloured regiments

Yellow 1624 (no c.o.)—25 Frans Bernhard v. Thurn —27 M. Teuffel —31 N. Brahe — 33 Lars Kagg —34 Schönbeck 1635 to France

Blue (from c.1634 called *The 'Old Blue'*) 1624 H. G. v. Arnim —25 M. Teuffel —27 H. v. der Noth —29 H. K. v. Klitzing —30 H. G. aus dem Winckel —36? 'Old Blue' 1650d

Red 1624/25 K. S. v. Plato —26 Ernhard Ehrenreiter —30 Giesebrecht v. Hogendorf — 35d

Green 1627 H. K. v. Klitzing —29 John Hepburn —32 Adam v. Pfuel —35d

New coloured regiments

Black 1629 D. v. Falkenberg —30d?

Black 1629 Adolf D. Efferen genannt Hall —31 G. Wulf v. Wildenstein —32d?

Black 1629 Claus Dietrich 'Sperreuter' —30? H. Jk. v. Thurn —34d

Black? 1630 Dodo Knyphausen —31d

Orange 1630 J. Vitzthum v. Eckstädt —35d

Brown 1630 Melchior v. Dargitz —31d?

White 1630 Damitz —31 J. Jost v. Rehn —32 W. Bürt —32 Dodo Knyphausen —37 Sarazini —38d

Key: First date is year of levying, following dates (e.g. '—32' = 1632) show changes of colonel; d = unit disbanded; v. = von; Christian names— M = Maximilian, S = Sigmund, W = Wilhelm, N = Nils, H = Hans, K = Kaspar, J = Johann, G = Georg, D = Dietrich, Jk = Jakob.

British Mercenaries

Most of Gustavus's foreign mercenaries were Germans, but he recruited many other nationalities. The Dutch and Flemish were sought after chiefly as engineers or artillerymen; the French (mostly

The brigade of three squadrons, from a print of the battle of Hessisch-Oldendorf (1633) in Theatrum Europaeum, III (Frankfurt, 1639). Each squadron was, in theory, made up of four companies (represented here by four company flags in front of each squadron's pikes). Low campaign strengths meant that, in practice, tactical squadrons almost always had more than four companies.
The Swedish brigade only barely outlived

Gustavus; Turner, who arrived in Germany in 1632, saw it used 'for one year after the King's death; but after that time, I saw it wear out when defensive arms first, and then pikes came to be neglected...' Brigades continued to be used as higher level groupings of regiments in the modern sense, but were replaced (except possibly in a few pitched battles) by a return to the squadron (i.e. battalion) as the tactical formation.

Huguenots) served often as dragoons; Protestant Bohemian exiles supplied at least one complete cavalry regiment. The British, however, outnumbered by a very large margin all these and other nationalities except the Germans. Their speciality was infantry, because the export of horses from Britain was forbidden.

The connection of Scotland with Sweden has often been called a 'special relationship'. The Scots and Swedes had much in common: harsh climates, poverty at home, and strict Protestantism. In a period when water linked rather than divided peoples they were not really so far apart geographically. When Gustavus had his main channels of mercenary recruitment from Germany cut off by enemy action in 1627 and 1628, it was only natural for him to turn to Britain for troops.

Soon, though, the Swedes began to appreciate the

Whereas the regiment and company were permanent structures, the 'Swedish' squadron and brigade were essentially temporary groupings for use on the battlefield. The Swedish squadron appeared first between 1617 and 1621. It was modelled on the Dutch battalion or half-regiment already used by the Dutch under Prince Maurits at the siege of Rhees in 1614. This diagram is based on one by Watts in The Swedish Discipline. *The*

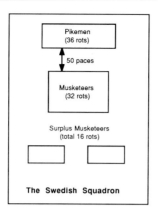

Pikemen
(36 rots)

50 paces

Musketeers
(32 rots)

Surplus Musketeers
(total 16 rots)

The Swedish Squadron

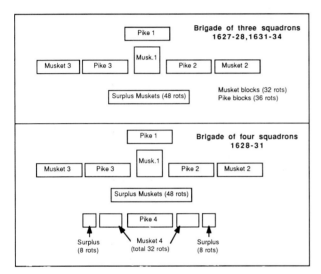

Pike 1

**Brigade of three squadrons
1627-28, 1631-34**

Musk.1

Musket 3 Pike 3   Pike 2   Musket 2

Surplus Muskets (48 rots)

Musket blocks (32 rots)
Pike blocks (36 rots)

Pike 1

**Brigade of four squadrons
1628-31**

Musk.1

Musket 3 Pike 3   Pike 2   Musket 2

Surplus Muskets (48 rots)

Pike 4

Surplus
(8 rots)   Musket 4   Surplus
           (total 32 rots)   (8 rots)

squadron deployed in two main bodies: a pike block of 36 rots (files of six men), followed after an interval (usually of 50 paces) by a musketeer formation of 32 rots. The squadron's musketeers could advance to either side of the pike block if it was threatened. A further 16 rots of 'surplus' musketeers (96 men) provided a reserve or could be detached for other duties. Excluding officers, a squadron numbered 504 marching men (half a full-strength regiment).

Gustavus did try to make the squadron a permanent unit: half-regiments of four companies were frequently referred to as 'squadrons' for administrative purposes—indeed, any undersize regiment of three to six companies was usually termed a squadron. But it is wrong to link these 'administrative' squadrons too closely with the 'tactical' one.

The 'Swedish' brigade is one of the few innovations that can be credited to Gustavus (or at least to his staff) with some certainty. Surviving contemporary sketches of orders of battle show that after trials with five and even seven squadron wedges, a three-squadron brigade evolved in Polish Prussia over 1627–28. Gustavus added a fourth (reserve) squadron in around 1628–29, probably to counter the huge Imperialist tercios he expected to face in Germany.

The only detailed diagram of the 'Swedish' brigade published in its day was Lord Reay's sketch in The Swedish Discipline *in 1632. This has led to the mistaken view that the brigade of four squadrons was the standard formation: it was, in fact, seldom used in battle, and had to be abandoned in mid-1631 because of a shortage of pikemen. The brigade of three squadrons took its place. Lord Reay (Col. Mackay) left Swedish service for Scotland late in 1630, and never returned, so was quite unaware of the changes that took place in 1631; his diagram was out of date before it was printed.*

It is important to understand the difference between Swedish brigades and regiments. Brigades were not permanent bodies. They were made

up at the start of a campaign from the manpower available. Sometimes there were enough men in a single regiment to field a complete brigade (as was at first the case with the Yellow and Blue Regiments); usually, though, as many as four or five regiments had to combine. The regiments still existed as separate entities within the brigade. When a brigade received heavy casualties or units were detached for garrison duties, new regiments were brought in to maintain the brigade as a viable battlefield formation.

The custom of giving brigades colour names has also caused much confusion—most famously in the case of the Green Regiment and the Green Brigade (or 'Scots' Brigade, as it was called briefly). According to The Swedish Intelligencer *(2, p. 28), brigades 'had their names from the chiefest Colours [flags] belonging to the eldest [i.e. senior] Colonell of the brigade.' In practice, a colour name was used only if the brigade included a coloured regiment; and then only if its flags were still recognisable and not completely in tatters. By 1632 this was seldom the case, and most brigades were called simply after the name of their senior colonel.*

British for positive reasons: 'They are good fellows, easier to deal with than others tend to be,' wrote Oxenstierna in 1630. Whereas German mercenaries had political interests too close to home, the British could be trusted to hold strategic Latvian, Prussian and North German garrisons. Scots, in particular, began to play a rôle out of all proportion to their numbers. The German mercenary and Swedish conscript units they were given to command easily outnumbered the wholly British units. At least a dozen Britons rose to the rank of major-general and higher, Field-Marshal Alexander Leslie being the most famous of all.

As perhaps the ultimate symbol of trust Mackay was commissioned in 1630/31 to raise a British 'Drabant' bodyguard for Gustavus. This only materialised shortly before the battle of Lützen, when officers from disbanded British regiments were formed into a makeshift royal bodyguard while awaiting further appointments.

Mackay has come down in modern histories as the most famous recruiting master, but his efforts were easily surpassed by those of Sir James Spens, who held at various times the curious status of British ambassador to Sweden and Swedish ambassador to Britain. As early as 1606 Spens was raising troops for Sweden. Between 1624 and 1629 alone he personally arranged the levying of six regiments in Britain. In 1629 he was appointed 'General over all the British' in Swedish service. He died in 1632, allegedly from the shock of Gustavus's death.

Many high-ranking Britons decided to stay on in Sweden, and some, like Spens, Hamilton, Forbes and Fleetwood, established important Swedish noble bloodlines. But with trouble brewing in Britain most returned home between 1638 and 1640. They brought back (especially to the Scots army) a much-needed professionalism; but also a brutal manner picked up in Germany that marred the otherwise fairly gentlemanly conduct of the English Civil Wars of the 1640s.

These veterans also left some of the most detailed accounts of Gustavus's wars available in any language. Robert Monro's *Expedition with the Worthy Scots Regiment (called Mac-Keyes Regiment)*... is justifiably famous as (probably) the first ever regimental history. James Turner, who arrived with Lumsdaine's new regiment in 1632 and stayed in Germany until 1639/40, left numerous practical insights in his *Memoirs* and *Pallas Armata*. William Watts, later military chaplain to Charles I and Prince Rupert, compiled in *The Swedish Intelligencer* and *The Swedish Discipline* eyewitness accounts from many British colonels including Hepburn, Muschamp, Astley and Mackay.

Table B: British Regiments in Swedish Service, levied 1624–32

Spens' Levies

1624–34?	J. Spens (*Scots*)
1627–34?	J. Ramsay (*Scots*)
1629–33?	G. Earl of Crawford (*Engl.*)
1629–36?	G. Cunningham (*Scots*)
1629–30	Jn. Meldrum (*Scots*)
1629–35?	Jn. Hamilton (*Scots*)

Donald Mackay's Levies

1629–34	D. Mackay, Lord Reay (*Scots*)
1629–31	Mackay (Monro's sqdrn) (*Scots*)
1631–33	John Monro (*Scots*)
1631–33	Thomas Conway (*Engl.*)

Alexander Forbes' Levies

1631–33?	A. Forbes (*Scots/Irish*)
1631–33?	F. Hamilton (*Scots/Irish*)

Marquis of Hamilton's 'English Army'

1631–32	A. Hamilton (*Scots*)
1631–32	J. Hamilton (*Engl.*)
1631–32	J. Ramsay (*Engl.*)
1631–32	J. Astley (*Engl.*)

Other Levies

1632–34?	Arthur Aston (*Engl.*)
1632–34?	J. Lumsdaine (*Scots*)
1632–39	G. Fleetwood (*Engl.*)

Levied from Scots in Polish/Danish service

1629–33?	R. ('Young') Leslie (*Scots*)
1629?–38/39	Patrick Ruthven (*Scots/Germans*)

Christian names: J = James/Jacob, Jn = John, A = Alexander, G = George, R = Robert, F = Frederick, D = Donald. Only regiments composed principally of British troops levied between 1624–32 are listed; several others were levied immediately before and after these dates.

INFANTRY ARMS AND ARMOUR

The musket was a latecomer to Sweden: it was already well established in northern Europe by the 1570s, but the first shipment of 200 muskets from Holland is recorded only in 1592. The Swedes were reluctant to give up their older but much handier light firearms—'small shot' or calivers, known in Sweden mostly as *rör* or *bösser*—and there was little pressing urgency, since Sweden's chief enemies in the Baltic were also slow to take up the musket.

The 'true' or 'full' musket was bored to fit lead balls weighing '8 to the pound' (about 21.7 mm), and fired smaller balls of '10 to the pound' to facilitate loading in battle. With a weight of about 7.5 kg and a ferocious recoil, this was considered by many (including Wallhausen) to be too burdensome for the average soldier.

In 1599 the Dutch had already introduced a new standard: bored for lead balls of '10 to the pound' (about 19.7 mm), it fired balls '12 to the pound rolling in' (about 18.6 mm) for field use. This was known in Sweden as the 'ordinary' or 'half' musket. Its weight was at first around 6–6.5 kg. The Swedes seem never to have fully abandoned the larger calibre: in 1626, for instance, Hoppe noted that in Polish Prussia they were carrying 'very large muskets'.

Lightening of the musket

It was often claimed that Gustavus was the first to lighten the musket so that it could be used without a rest. As late as 1631, however, he placed an order with the Flemish director of the Swedish arms industry, Louis de Geer, to outfit 32 complete infantry regiments: all were to be equipped with musket forks. The inventories of the Stockholm Arsenal make it clear that forks were still being issued many years after Gustavus's death: 1626—5,300; 1635—12,162; 1645—826; 1655—none.

Lighter muskets, however, had already begun to appear in Europe. Stocks were redesigned to be smaller, and barrels, which made up most of the musket's weight, were lightened considerably by improved casting techniques. Some, probably with shortened barrels, found their way into Swedish hands apparently from captured German arsenals. In 1632, Sebastian Dehner, chronicler of the German town of Rothenburg ob der Tauber, wrote: '6 May… a company of Swedish infantry arrived, among them were musketeers armed with the new very light muskets without forks.'

Abolition of the Bandolier

Modern historians have claimed that Gustavus abolished the bandolier and introduced cartridge pouches for his musketeers. Again, there is no evidence for this, and more to contradict it. The Stockholm Arsenal, in fact, continued to issue bandoliers until at least 1670.

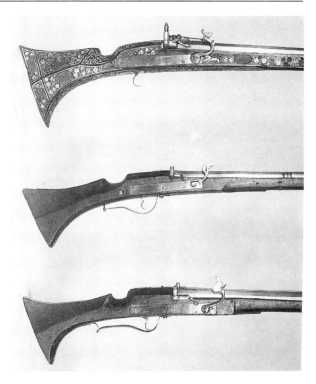

Matchlock muskets with the 'fishtail' Spanish–Dutch butt, the standard type in Gustavus's army. Precise dating is still difficult; the best clues are weight and calibre. The barrel length also gives a hint of nationality: in Sweden this was set at 2 Swedish ells/4 Swedish ft. (118.7 cm, 3 ft. 10¾ in.), but most surviving weapons are slightly shorter—according to a document of 1629, barrel makers would only be fined if their barrels were 3 'fingers' (5 cm, 2 in.) too short.
Top: Dutch parade musket c.1600 (AM 4032); middle: Swedish munition musket with 'crowned ring' mark of Jönköping, c.1620–40 (4.1 kg, and 115.5 cm long barrel of 20 mm calibre, AM 4062); bottom: Swedish? musket c.1600–30 (6.4 kg, with 114 cm barrel of 19.1 mm calibre, AM 4064). (Royal Army Museum, Stockholm— hereafter, AM)

Turner, however, writing about his Swedish service in the 1630s, noted: '… I saw these [Bandoliers] laid aside in some German armies: for it is impossible for soldiers wanting Cloaks (and more want Cloaks than have any) to keep safe these flasks… from snow and rain, which soon spoils them, and makes the powder altogether useless.'

Swinesfeathers

The main reason for the early failures of the Swedes against the Poles was their shortage of the pikemen

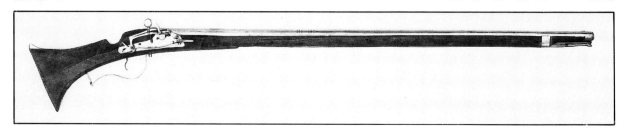

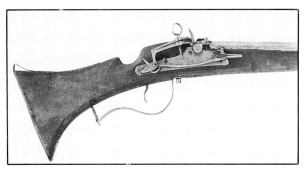

Musket with a Swedish snaplock (early flintlock). They were issued in bulk in the 1620s, and not just to artillery and bodyguards as in other armies; this was partly because of difficulties in Sweden of obtaining the huge quantities of match needed for matchlock weapons. As early as 1621 Wallhausen thought them 'discardable antiquities', and recommended more reliable matchlocks in their place; Gustavus made great efforts to replace them for the 1630s. Calibre 19.6 mm, barrel length 118.5 cm. Proofmarks suggest manufacture at Jönköping in the 1620s. (Wrangel Armoury, Skokloster)

essential to protect them from the fierce Polish cavalry. 'The infantry are very badly furnished with long pikes and harness,' wrote Johann of Nassau; 'also they can and will not be persuaded otherwise.'

Johann adopted an interesting stop-gap. He 'prepared a few hundred carts and had five pikes laid on and made fast to each one; these were pushed out in front of each formation… In use against cavalry they were found to be very good, and they were taken along into the field, since one could shoot over them and the exposed shooters could be covered with them.' These carts were still mentioned in Sweden in 1604, but soon fell out of use. (Johann, of course, demonstrated them again to Gustavus in 1620.)

There are already (possibly spurious) references to swinesfeathers in Gyllenhielm's 1601 account of his campaigns in Livonia, where he ordered his infantry to carry 4–4½ ft. long stakes with spikes at each end as 'swinesfeathers or Spanish Reiters' to be used against the Polish cavalry. By Gustavus's day they appear to have been forgotten, however.

Swinesfeathers (or 'Swedish feathers', as they were often called by foreign authors in later decades) were not, as usually suggested, invented by Gustavus, and in fact were not even Swedish: in 1618 Gustavus had been writing to one of Prince Maurits's teachers, Simon Stevin, in Holland to find out information about them. They were clearly derived from 'Spanish Reiters' ('Spanish horse') or *chevaux-de-frise* ('Frisian horses') used earlier in the Netherlands. In 1621 Gustavus ordered 16,000 swinesfeathers from his Arboga foundry—enough for 28 regiments. The first deliveries from the Stockholm Arsenal were made only in 1624. Anything between one and eight

A bandolier made from dark grey sealskin, from the Wrangel Armoury. Inventories suggest that it dates to before 1656. Each wooden powder container is 116 mm tall and covered with black leather to protect it from rain and to reduce noise. The bullet pouch and priming flask (sixth from the left, with a spout) have both fallen off and have been tied on incorrectly. Such priming flasks of the same pattern as ordinary powder containers are sometimes called 'corporals' in Swedish sources. They appear in the 1610s, and seem to have replaced the old triangular priming flasks by the 1630s. (Skokloster)

companies of an eight-company regiment were equipped with them, but not all regiments received them.

Turner describes them as: 'a stake five or six foot long, and about four finger thick, with a piece of sharp Iron nail'd to each end of it'. The most complete account is by Schildknecht, an engineer in Polish service, in his manual *Harmonia Fortalitiis*:

'In the Year [16]26 the Swedish musketeers... used against our Poles, instead of forks, a stick that was strong, long and thick... furnished at the front with a spike two spans long, and at the back with an iron barb, and called a "Schweinsfeder". During a charge the musketeers planted these Swinesfeathers firmly in the ground, obliquely towards our Polish cavalry, so that the spike pointed directly at the horse's chest. They stepped back somewhat and also gave fire over them... This fashion was used on the Swedish side for barely two years: why they stopped it I do not know. Perhaps it was because of the difficulty of carrying them, or that they did not always have to fight against cavalry... It astonished me, even at the time, that such an advantage against the cavalry should be allowed to go...'

Despite Schildknecht's note to the contrary, it is clear from arsenal inventories and numerous other sources that they were issued in addition to musket rests and not instead of them.

The origin of the term swinesfeather is unclear. It could be a slang term, meaning roughly 'pig-sticker', or it could be related to the boarspear. A connection has recently been suggested with the 'svinhufvud' (swine-head), which may be the old Swedish word for another anti-cavalry device—the caltrop.

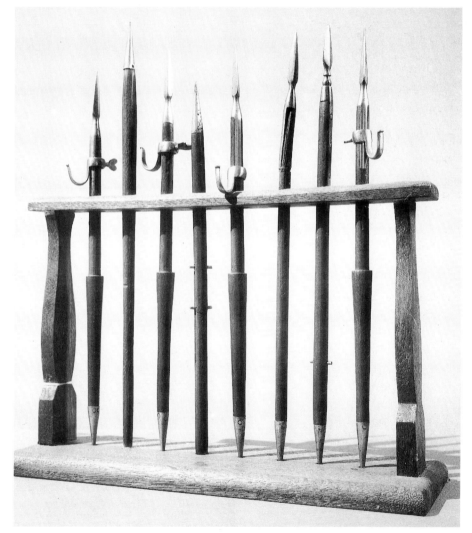

Models (approx. 1/6th scale) of 'Swedish feathers' and stakes for constructing chevaux-de-frise, *made as part of a complete miniature armoury by the Nuremberg engineer Johann Carl (active 1625–65). The proportions are distorted so that the shafts look thicker than the full size objects. It is usually said that Johann Carl made them for Gustavus during his stay in Nuremberg in 1632, but this is unlikely.*

Gustavus's infantry had already abandoned the swinesfeather in 1628, though there may have been a revival in the later 1630s after the pike arm was run down, since Turner claimed to 'have seen them made use of in Germany'. Turner also wrote (speculatively) of 'an instrument that might serve for both rest and feather, and such would perhaps be very useful and convenient.' Other descriptions make it clear that the musket-rest-cum-swinesfeather credited to Gustavus had, in fact, not yet been invented. These models were probably made in the 1650s or 1660s. (Germanisches Nationalmuseum, Nuremberg)

The partisan was the Swedish infantry officer's symbol of rank and his main battlefield weapon. Six partisans were issued per company, according to instructions dated 1623 and c.1630; it is not certain how these were distributed, but since there is no evidence for issues of halberds two of them may have gone to sergeants (who elsewhere in Europe used halberds), while the captain may have obtained his finer model elsewhere. (A) Swedish partisan c.1580–1600, probably a reworked halberd (LRK 25/407); (B) 1604–11, with Karl IX's initials CRS, probably made in Eskilstuna (LRK 2361); (C) mass-produced partisan made in Arboga for junior officers, 1620–35 (Hallwylska Museet); (D) quality 1620s Dutch partisan belonging to Nils Brahe (Skokloster); (E) partisan for the King's Bodyguard (Drabants) made in Amsterdam in 1626 (LRK 3767a). After Seitz, Bardisanen, (Stockholm, 1943).

Arsenal inventories, orders to arms manufacturers, and other sources prove that Swedish musketeers as well as pikemen were issued throughout Gustavus's reign with helmets. Wallhausen noted in 1615 that the best infantry helmets were to be found in the Netherlands. At first they were imported to Sweden from Holland; but by the late 1620s Swedish foundries began to mass produce 'Dutch pots' or 'storm-hats' such as this one under Dutch and Flemish supervision. Note the plume-holder at rear. Metal cheek pieces are missing from this example. (Photo: AM)

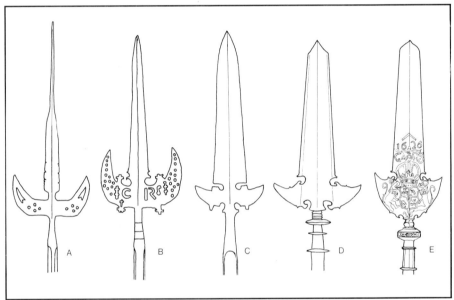

The Pike and Pikemen's Armour

There were two main types of pikehead popular at this period: a broad, flat lozenge, and a spike of square cross-section. Wallhausen wrote that the broad variety was generally thought better, but he found the square-head type was 'not bad against cavalry'. It is interesting, considering the Swedish obsession with cavalry defence, that nearly all surviving pikes in Sweden are of the square type. These pikes have the usual metal strips running down 50 to 100 cm on either side of the shaft from the pikehead. The pikeshafts are 3.5 cm in diameter at the thickest part, and taper towards both ends. They were made usually from ash wood, but Gustavus also permitted maple, pine and aspen.

The few surviving Swedish pikes that have not been drastically shortened in recent years to overcome storage problems are between 5.2 metres (17 ft.) and 5.4 metres (17 ft. 8 in.) long. This ties in well with the regulation 9 Swedish ells (5.3 metres) that Gustavus established in 1616. However, pikes often did not remain this length on campaign. Officers like Monro complained, apparently, to little effect about pikemen who 'cut off the lengths of their pikes as often seen upon marches, being very uncomely to see a squadron of pikes not all of one length'.

Gustavus placed special stress on the equipping of his pikemen. They were issued with full armour (harness), usually comprising back and breastplates, gorget, tassets for the thighs and helmet. After

Gustavus's death, lacking his personal supervision, the pike arm became increasingly run down, and the proportion of pikemen began to drop significantly as entire regiments converted themselves into musketeers.

In 1635 Chancellor Oxenstierna wrote that it was no longer necessary to send pike harness to Germany as they were little used and tended to get thrown away on the long marches typical of the campaign; the fall in issues of pike harness in the late 1630s is confirmed in the Stockholm Armoury inventories. By 1640 fully armoured pikemen must have been a rare sight in the Swedish army in Germany.

Infantry Swords

The swords of the ordinary infantrymen pose something of a problem, since none can be identified in Swedish collections. They differed from cavalry and officers' swords (which will be covered in the second of these *Men-at-Arms* titles) in being simpler and of poorer quality. In theory all native Swedish troops, both pikemen and musketeers, had to provide themselves with swords out of their 'file-money'. In practice, though, probably because enough were never available, many served without them— Hoppe's descriptions of native Swedish troops in Prussia in 1626 indicate that many had axes rather than swords. In 1630 Gustavus had all the 'file-money' paid directly to him; swords thereafter were delivered centrally.

INFANTRY UNIFORMS AND CLOTHING

The first thing that emerges from the account books is that buffcoats, sleeveless or otherwise, were not normally issued in Gustavus's army. They may have been worn on a fairly large scale among wealthy Dutch and German citizen militias; but among Swedish field armies they were probably used only by some officers, and then as private purchases or booty. The dress of the ordinary infantryman was a woollen cloth suit comprising breeches and a jacket, and

called simply 'soldier's clothing'. It was often issued in the form of cloth which had to be made up at the regiment's own expense. Cloth was seen as a basic necessity and, indeed, was often issued by the same officials responsible for army victuals.

New clothing was normally issued once a year, just before the onset of winter. It comprised shoes, socks and shirts in addition to the basic jacket and breeches. The Swedes were, understandably, particularly concerned about winter clothing. Swedish peasants were told to make 'voluntary' contributions of furs and woollen socks and shoes for the Latvian campaign in 1621/2; and warm Russian boots were purchased in Riga. A Scots regiment in December 1625 were ordered to garrison Riga only 'if the Scots have sufficiently warm clothes to stand the cold'. During the German campaigns, too, there were regular shipments from Sweden of 'Lappish' furs for the army.

Though the basic purpose of keeping soldiers clothed was for decency and warmth, Gustavus had certainly begun to see already the incidental benefits that good clothing of a single colour and cut gave in the field. It was already common to have military clothing made in a standardised style. A 'pattern' (probably a finished garment) was often sent to the tailor along with the order. Military garments, in Sweden at least, were already quite distinct from everyday peasant dress, and indeed from most other civilian clothing. The hoary old statement that Thirty Years' War soldiers simply wore their ordinary civilian clothing is simply not true.

In a letter dated May 1621, Gustavus wrote that new Swedish conscripts should not arrive 'in their farm habits and with their long jackets', since the many foreigners in Stockholm would see them and spread spiteful rumours abroad 'to the kingdom's greatest despair and damage'. He recommended that these conscripts obtain dress 'befitting men of war'. He also made it clear that 'the material itself matters little, only that the clothes are well cut'. And as early as 1622, he ordered that each company or regiment should be similarly dressed.

Uniform colours

Until about 1620 the majority of soldiers in Sweden (particularly first-time conscripts who purchased clothing with the 'file-money' levied on conscription)

Musketeer from the engraved metal coffin of Erik Soop, colonel of the Västergötland cavalry regiment, made for his funeral in 1632. The musketeer wears a small jacket, baggy breeches and a hat with a round crown. He carries a musket with a rather odd-looking stock, used with a rest and bandolier. Such engravings were usually copied from foreign prints, and were often many years out of date. (Skara Cathedral, sketch after Bellander)

Musketeer on engraved back-panel of a clock, marked 1631, made probably at Ulm in south Germany. The shoulder 'wings' of his newly fashionable long-skirted jacket are worth noting. (Skokloster)

had to make do with the locally produced cloth. This coarse woollen material, called 'vadmal' in Sweden, was usually undyed and so of a greyish-white colour, the exact shade depending on the sheep of the area. This 'peasant grey' cloth was regarded in Sweden almost as a symbol of class. Coloured cloth (broadcloth)—the material of the upper classes—was mostly imported from Holland, England or Germany; and because of its great expense was reserved for royal bodyguards, and for specific issues of uniforms for state occasions such as royal visits. The Swedish clothing industry was not yet sufficiently developed to produce enough coloured cloth for the everyday use of the army as a whole.

Gustavus seems first to have become anxious about his army's poor clothing during his visit to Germany in 1620. In Germany and Holland complete regiments of 'yellow coats' and 'red coats' had been common since 1600 and earlier. On his return, he decided on a cheap measure to add colour to otherwise drab garments by adding coloured trimmings, probably inserted in the seams. A letter to the king dated 24 September 1620 mentions that: '… cloth for the soldiers will not be sufficient for all companies. The Småland infantry have been sent enough for 100 "riding-jackets" with yellow and blue trimmings, the Ostgoth infantry enough for 350 "riding-jackets" of "in-mixed" [insprengtt] cloth and yellow trimmings, and the Uppland regiment… 250 "riding-jackets" with yellow and black trim.'

The real solution, however, was both to improve native cloth production, and to import more cloth. This was achieved to some extent in the early 1620s when the infantry began to enjoy regular annual issues of a coarse coloured cloth called 'piuk', and the officers received fine English cloth. But the system was far from efficient. In July 1626, when Gustavus landed in Polish Prussia, Hoppe saw the first columns march into Marienberg: 'The foot were mostly shabby Swedish peasants, they had poor clothing but were disciplined soldiers…'. Poles like the chronicler Pawel Piasecki thought much the same: 'they were more like labourers than soldiers'. Even Gustavus admitted (in a letter copied by Hoppe) that 'These men I have with me now, are only poor Swedish farmhands and poor in appearance, also ill clothed, but they fight well, and I hope that they will shortly be better clothed; already before Frauenburg they have obtained 500 red coats.'

Gustavus was most fortunate in taking Elbing without a fight; the Baltic base of the English Eastland Company, Elbing was the unloading point of large shipments of English cloth bound for Poland. This was of great help during the Polish campaigns.

In 1626 he decided to improve clothing manufacture at home. The clothmills of Sweden were to deliver their output direct to the Royal Wardrobe (Klädkammaren); and a central workshop was to be set up in Stockholm employing 40 to 50 tailors who were to provide ready-made suits of clothing to his troops. They were to make 'Hungarian jackets' (jackor) in two sizes: two-thirds of them large, and one-third small. Unfortunately, it is difficult to tell to what extent if any these projects were carried out, because the Royal Wardrobe account books for 1626 and 1627 are missing.

Uniforms of the Coloured Regiments

No Swedish regulations have yet been found that required coloured regiments to wear uniforms of the same colour as their names. In Denmark, however, in 1625, the Red Regiment and Blue Regiment wore 'casaques' of red and light blue respectively. The date here is significant, because it was exactly the same year in which the Swedish coloured regiments began to appear.

Contemporary descriptions (mostly by Hoppe—see commentaries to Plates D and F) show that at least the Yellow, Blue and Red Regiments had coats of a colour matching their names; but no references have been found for the other coloured regiments.

A report of October 1627 (PRO London, SP 95/2/f. 179) from James Spens to Charles I of England seems to refer specifically to the first four colour regiments: 'For clothing his armie he [Gustavus] hath coarse cloth made in his countrie;... and with this he clothes his common soldiers, causing to dye it in red, yellow, green and blue, which makes a great show in the fields; and this was never done before this king's time.' Of course, Spens was writing only about the situation in Sweden, but it was probably this very passage (quoted first by Walter Harte in 1759) that started the rumour that Gustavus invented the uniform.

Even non-coloured regiments do seem on the whole to have received uniforms of a single colour. The accounts, however, refer only to 'coloured cloth', and rarely specify the shade. It would seem that those responsible delivered one colour if they had enough

Though the Thirty Years' War produced a flood of pictures, it is difficult to identify troops who are Swedish. Most artists painting the Thirty Years' War were actually based in Holland and Belgium. Those from Germany lived mostly in the wealthy towns of Nuremberg, Augsburg and Frankfurt, and they mostly copied the troops they saw every day—namely citizen militias, which usually wore civilian clothing. This has greatly distorted our idea of what Thirty Years' War soldiers actually wore. Even this *carefully selected group of contemporary images is far from 100% reliable. (A) Swedish musketeers at storm of Würzburg, Oct. 1631, by Georg Köler of Nuremberg; (B) Gustavus's entry into Erfurt, Oct. 1631, from sketch by Samuel Fritz (town archives, Erfurt); (C) Royal Lifeguards? at Steinheim, Nov. 1631, probably by Merian of Frankfurt; (D) musketeer with Monmouth cap? from woodcut of Gustavus's entry into Augsburg, April 1632, by Georg Kress of Augsburg.*

of it, but were not afraid of mixing if they did not: references to 'any-colour-at-hand cloth' are common. This rather offhand attitude must have given some companies the appearance of harlequins: in 1629, for example, the 106 soldiers of John Ruthven's newly arrived Scots company of James Ramsay's regiment received the following cloth: 39 ells of red, 42 ells of yellow, 351 ells of Scots kersey (grey or perhaps blue), 113 ells of unspecified colour, and 207 ells of 'anycoloured cloth'.

The German campaigns

The question still remains: to what extent was Gustavus's army uniformed in Germany? If one thing is certain, it is that Gustavus determined his troops would make a better show than they had in Poland. Chancellor Oxenstierna managed to buy cloth from the English Eastland Company in Elbing on credit, and with this he had clothed most of the new mercenaries assembling in Prussia by early 1630. Back in Sweden, Gustavus realised that the arrangements for equipping his conscripts locally would never work properly. In January 1630 he ordered that the 'file-money' raised on conscription should be handed over to his officials and he would himself issue

clothing. This measure worked, at least while he was in Sweden to supervise it: virtually all the new conscripts and mercenaries assembling in Sweden in early 1630 were issued with clothing by the Royal Wardrobe.

After the landings in Germany the Swedes continued to purchase cloth on a large scale; in 1631, for example, 3,803 men of Swedish national regiments received ready-made suits of clothing in Stettin, a transaction again co-ordinated by the Royal Wardrobe.

Despite the hardships of the first year's campaigning the Swedes managed to maintain a fairly decent appearance. On 15 September, a few days before the battle of Breitenfeld, when the Elector of Saxony (whose own fresh army was immaculately uniformed) inspected the Swedes, he found them 'Not nearly as bad as We were led to believe…'. Gualdo Priorato, who served at one time in both opposing armies, noted of Gustavus's infantry at Breitenfeld that 'the greater part of the soldiers [probably meaning only the front line of four brigades] were clad in blue and yellow casacks'.

'Better men… nor better cloathed did I ever see,' wrote the British envoy Henry Vane when he watched the main Swedish army leave Würzburg two months later. By this time they had benefited from the success of Breitenfeld, in particular the huge captured stores at Würzburg, from which few units were said to have departed without new clothing.

Again in the following year, after careful examination under the floorboards of the Munich arsenal,

The casack or casaque was a mysterious garment often mentioned in written sources. In 1621 Wallhausen called it 'Schützenrock [shooter's-coat] or cosacken', and it seems he was referring to a tabard-like coat of the type shown here in Peter Iselburg's Neues Soldaten Buchlein of 1615 (lifted from de Gheyn). Later versions may have differed considerably. Wallhausen described it as the only garment a musketeer needed, because it could protect bandoliers and musket from rain (by hiding the barrel in a sleeve!). The main disadvantage was cost, since it needed more cloth than breeches and jacket; this may explain why references to it are rare in Sweden. Orders for casacks became slightly more common after the Swedes arrived in Germany. The Italians Deodati and Gualdo Priorato write that most Swedes at Breitenfeld and Lützen wore 'casacche', but it is hard to find these casacks on pictures of the 1630s, and possible that the word now meant little more than a jacket. (PAN Library, Gdansk)

The road to war – native Swedish troops 1626
1 Corporal of musketeers
2 Pikeman 4 Drummer
3 Captain   5 Musketeer, colonel's squadron

A

The Eastern Front: Finns and Lapps
1 Finnish musketeer
2 Lapp, reindeer and sledge

B
1
2

Storming the breach –
British mercenaries 1631
1 Pikeman, Mackay's/Monro's
Scottish Regiment
2 English musketeer,
Hamilton's Army
3 Irish musketeer, Alexander
Hamilton's Scottish Regiment
4 Irish/Highland 'redshanks' recruit

3

4

1

C

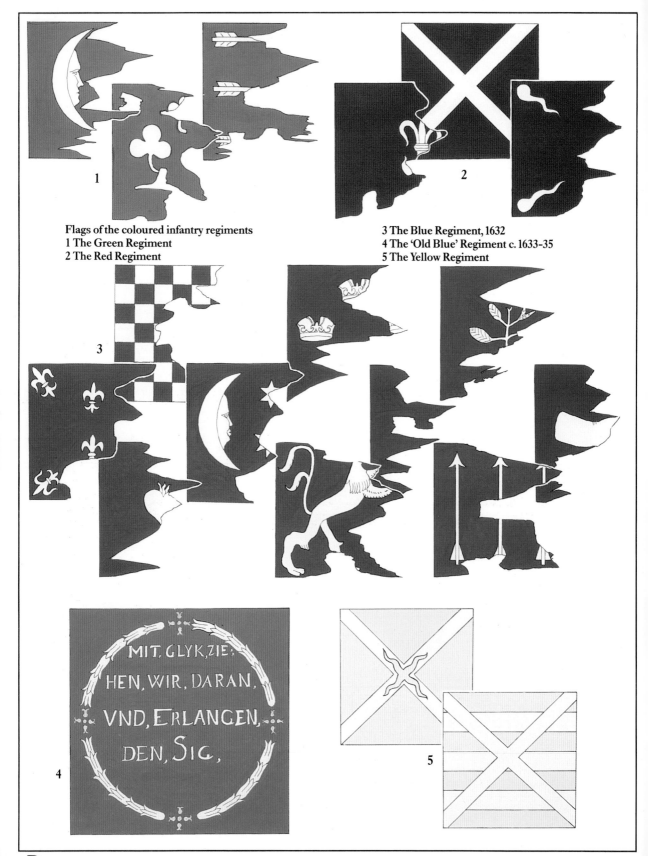

Flags of the coloured infantry regiments
1 The Green Regiment
2 The Red Regiment

3 The Blue Regiment, 1632
4 The 'Old Blue' Regiment c. 1633-35
5 The Yellow Regiment

MIT, GLYK, ZIE;
HEN, WIR, DARAN,
VND, ERLANGEN,
DEN, SIG,

D

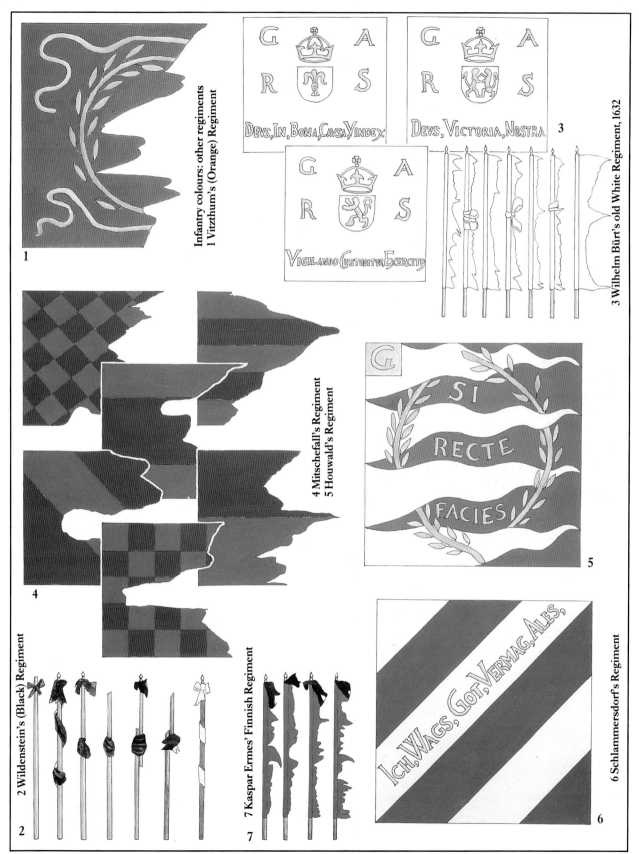

Infantry colours: other regiments

1 Vitzthum's (Orange) Regiment

DEVS, IN, BONA, CAVSA, VINDEX

DEVS, VICTORIA, NOSTRA

3

VIGILANDO CUSTODITVR EXERCITO

3 Wilhelm Bürt's old White Regiment, 1632

4 Mitschefall's Regiment
5 Houwald's Regiment

SI RECTE FACIES

5

2 Wildenstein's (Black) Regiment

7 Kaspar Ermes' Finnish Regiment

6 Schlammersdorf's Regiment

ICH, WAGS, GOT, VERMAG, ALES,

E

1   3   2

The Old Guard: The Yellow Regiment at Lützen, 1632
1 & 2 Musketeer and Pikeman, Yellow Regiment
3 'Commanded' musketeer, Yellow Regiment
4 Musketeer, King's Lifeguard company
5 Ensign, King's Lifeguard company
6 Colonel, Yellow Regiment

Destitution: North Germany and Prussia, 1634/5
1 Swedish peasant recruit
2 Swedish musketeer, 1633 mourning uniform
3 Veteran wearing Hongreline

G

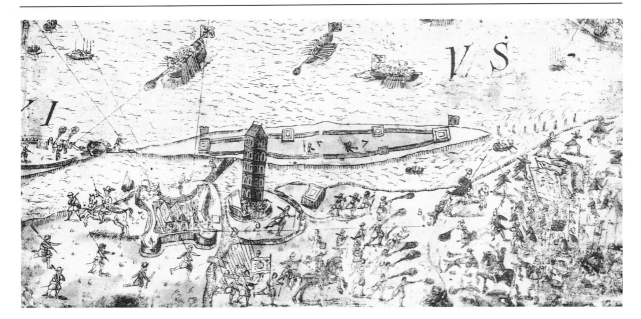

The siege of Riga, 1621. On the right are the Poles-Lithuanians in long Eastern garments, and on the left the Swedes in small jackets and baggy breeches. Note that the Swedish musketeers wear morion-type helmets and carry short calivers with curved butts rather than muskets. The flag on the lower left bears an orb, a typical emblem found on Swedish flags. Detail of a print by Georg Schwengl, a citizen of Riga who went on to become an engineer in Swedish service. (AM)

according to Monro, 'were found clothes and Armes, ready to cloth an army of ten thousand foote, which helped our Army much.' But things were beginning to change for the worse. Cloth stocks in Sweden and northern Germany had been seriously depleted as the Swedish army marched south. Gustavus wrote as early as November 1631 demanding that the new regiments mustering in Sweden 'should not be sent to us, naked from the neck down as has been the case until now'.

With the Swedish army growing at a phenomenal rate after the victory at Breitenfeld, even the wealthiest areas of Germany, around Frankfurt-am-Main, could not hope to clothe all the new mercenaries, let alone provide the veterans with the customary winter clothing.

In the chaos that followed Gustavus's death the soldiers in southern Germany were not being paid, let alone issued with new uniforms; and with the army halted in its tracks there were no new stocks to capture, so the clothing situation degenerated even further. The raggamuffin armies on Thirty Years' War battle paintings are mostly those of the later 1630s, from a time when the Swedes (meaning usually German Protestants under Swedish control) became almost legendary for their scruffiness, and when in the Czech language 'Szwed' became synonymous with a man in rags.

Conclusions

For a long time it was believed that Gustavus invented the military uniform. In fact, he was only copying what others had done before him elsewhere in Europe. The suits of clothing he issued were often uniform both in colour and in cut, but the motivation was mostly to cut costs. With the coloured regiments, though, there is good evidence that he was trying to go beyond basic necessity and was attempting to create a unit identity based partly on uniform. But this, too, was not his idea: it had already been done by the Danes among others.

There is, however, some vague and potentially controversial evidence that Gustavus was trying to standardise on blue uniforms for his native Swedish regiments—blue, of course, was adopted only much later in the 17th century as the standard Swedish coat colour. A 'New Blue Swedish regiment' of Ostgoths was recorded by Hoppe in Prussia in 1628; and several native Swedish units in Germany were on occasion described as 'blue' regiments—most notably Erik Hand's Ostgoth Regiment, which may be the same as Hoppe's 'New Blue Regiment'. Two

Table C: The Infantry Brigades, early September 1631

No of Coys.	Regiment	Pikemen	Musketeers	Officers
	The Yellow Brigade			
I	King's Lifeguard company	48	60	22
12	The Yellow Regt. (Teuffel)	514	690	192
4	Chemnitz	42	120	64
		604		
	The Blue Brigade			
12	The Blue Regt. (Winckel)	384	636	192
12	The Red Regt.	189	386	192
		573		
	Åke Oxenstierna's Brigade (Swedes/Finns)			
8	Lillie *Uppland, Närke & Värmland*	135	330	128
8	Hastfehr *Finns*	132	294	128
7	Oxenstierna *Dalarna*	324	516	128
		591		
	Erik Hand's Swedish Brigade			
8	Erik Hand *Östergötland*	348	540	128
4	W. von Salzburg *Dalsland*	168	282	64
8	Carl Hård *Västergötland*	120	240	128
		636		

brigades at Breitenfeld and one at Lützen were made up entirely of native Swedes, and contemporary descriptions suggest that on both occasions they were mostly dressed in blue. Blue cloth was also ordered more commonly than other colours: in 1631, for example, Hans Barkhusen was contracted by the Swedish state to buy 20,000 ells of cloth overseas, preferably dyed blue, but if he was unable to find enough then red or brown.

Note:

Brigades were not permanent structures; their com-ponent regiments were often changed to keep the number of pikemen close to a fixed number—648 pikemen—for three-squadron brigades (as here). The eight brigades above were reorganised into seven for the battle of Breitenfeld on 17 September; some regiments were even split (for the battle only) between different brigades.

Von Thurn's brigade demonstrates most clearly that regiments were not organised into brigades simply because they had the same colour flags or uniforms. Note also that each regiment, no matter how depleted, has its full complement of officers.

No of Coys.	Regiment	Pikemen	Musketeers	Officers
	The Green Brigade			
8	The Green Regt. (Hepburn)	244	457	128
8	Monro of Foulis *Germans*	150	360	128
–	Mitschefall	66	264	128
8	Bock	–	546	128
		460		
	The Scots Brigade			
8	James Lumsdaine (ex-Spens)	180	300	128
8	Mackay/Monro	144	252	128
8	James Ramsay	108	327	128
8	John Hamilton	72	336	128
		504		
	Von Thurn's Brigade			
8	Count von Thurn (Black)	103	241	128
8	Hall von Efferen (Black)	84	330	128
12	Damitz (White Regt.)	144	426	192
8	Vitzthum (Orange Regt.)	270	372	128
8	Dargitz (Brown Regt.)	96	216	128
		697		
	?'s Brigade			
12	Rosen	156	411	192
8	Waldstein	180	366	128
–	John Ruthven *Germans*	177	350	128
		513		
	Musketeer Reserve			
8	General Banér's Regt.	–	810	128

THE PLATES

A: The road to war—native Swedish troops, 1626

Native Swedes formed the backbone of Gustavus's army during his early campaigns. The men shown here from the Norrland *Landsregiment* are based on the Duwall portrait of 1626. Note, however, that most Swedish native troops at this time do not appear to have been as well uniformed as shown here; descriptions of them in Prussia in 1626 suggest an appearance more like the Swedish peasant recruit in Plate G.

A1: Corporal of musketeers

An interesting feature of the uniforms of Gustavus's army was that jackets and breeches were often of the same colour, because they were usually made from a single issue of cloth. The accounts of the Royal Wardrobe (*Klädkammaren*) at the Slottsarkivet, Stockholm, as well as the army account books in the Krigsarkivet and elsewhere, describe in great detail

The views through the windows of this fairly uninspiring portrait are the most detailed surviving pictures of Gustavus's native troops. A coat of arms with the date 1626 has allowed Arné Danielsson to identify the officer as Col. Jakob Duwall, and hence his troops as the Norrland Landsregiment. Duwall (lived 1589–1634) was a north German who claimed descent from the Scottish MacDougalls. Gilded chains (here with an unusually early portrait medallion of Gustavus) were given to officers as rewards for good service. The portrait is signed NF P: possibly the Frenchman Nicolas de la Fage. (Karlberg Slott, Stockholm)

might began to prevail. The gorget is probably worn as a sign of rank, suggesting a corporal.

The source shows a firearm with an old-fashioned downward curving butt: probably an obsolete caliver rather than a musket—a shortage of muskets forced the Swedes to continue using calivers as late as 1630. The caliver was light enough not to need a musket rest, but Wallhausen suggested (in 1615) that it was best 'to accustom calivermen to carry the fork with their caliver; it will be for them a gentle exercise for later carrying the musket.'

A2: Pikeman

Pikemen wore the same uniforms as musketeers, but it is difficult to make out much detail of their equipment on the Duwall portrait. Fortunately, there is a suit of pikeman's armour at Duwall's feet on his portrait (possibly the colonel's own suit).

A3: Captain

Swedish officers were often issued with cloth at the same time as their men. They received more than their soldiers (for example: ordinary soldiers, musicians and corporals in James Scott's Finnish regiment in 1632 received 5 ells, other NCOs 6, lieutenants and ensigns 8, and captains 12). It was also of better quality (often English broadcloth), and the officers' higher pay allowed them to have it tailored more fashionably. White plumes appear to have been standard for the entire *landsregiment*. The officers in each row (i.e. administrative squadron) on the source wear a common sash colour: orange here, or grey-green in the 'colonel's' squadron. As will be discussed more fully in Volume 2, there is, in fact, virtually no evidence at all for a national Swedish sash colour during Gustavus's lifetime. This captain carries a good quality imported Dutch partisan as his symbol of rank; partisans issued to junior officers were manufactured in Sweden and of much poorer quality.

these issues of cloth for uniforms. Over 1628–32 the typical amount for an ordinary soldier was 4 to 5 Swedish ells. The greater part was for breeches rather than jackets. In 1632, for example, Sperling's Södermanland regiment received red and blue cloth and was instructed to use 2.5 ells for jacket and 2.75 for breeches; this meant that the jackets were quite small and tight. Any extra cloth allowance would be used on lengthening the skirt of the jacket.

The helmets on the source resemble a type of morion common at around 1600 in Protestant Germany, and hint at the strong Swedish links with Germany (especially Lübeck) before Dutch trading

Detail from the Duwall portrait of 12 of the 24 companies of the Norrland Landsregiment in 1626. Each row of four companies has uniformly clothed men and officers, suggesting that each represents an administrative squadron. The flags are of the small Dutch style (approx. 1.75 metres square) issued 1622–29, which replaced an even smaller pattern (approx. 1.65 metres square) issued 1621–22. The flags have been over-painted, perhaps reflecting this change. They are, from left row to right: red, green, yellow, all with gold wreaths; one flag has a lion and crossed swords or arrows.

37

Drummers from the Duwall portrait. This is one of the earliest known representations of sleeved buffcoats. Few ordinary infantrymen outside of town militias wore buffcoats at this period; these were probably purchased privately by the colonel.

A4: Drummer

Each infantry company was allowed three drummers. Experienced and intelligent men were often preferred to boys as they had a secondary rôle as messengers, and had to act on their initiative and take in all they saw if this job took them behind enemy lines. The silver-braided buffcoat has been restored from pictures of Dutch militia (*schutter*) companies, and the double-ended drumsticks are taken from a German print of a Thirty Years' War drummer.

A5: Musketeer, colonel's squadron

This musketeer is typical of those in the row of four companies closest to Duwall on the portrait. This position and the more decorative dress suggest it to be from the colonel's 'administrative squadron'. The swinesfeather is reconstructed from eyewitness accounts; swinesfeathers were issued from 1624 until 1628 in addition to musket rests.

B: The Eastern Front: Finns and Lapps

The Scandinavians have used skis for thousands of years. Norse mythology had its own ski war god, Ull, stepson of Thor, and a ski goddess, Skade. One saga even records the 11th-century King Harald Hadrada boasting of his skill at skiing.

Ski-troops were certainly in use in Sweden–Finland in the 1500s; by the 1600s references to them are common. The first recorded captain of ski-troops was the Finn Hans Boije; in March 1606 he crossed the frozen Gulf of Finland to Narva with 600 skiers. Widekindi writes, in 1671, of 4,000 Swedish ski-troops sent to assist the Russians against Poland in 1609. This figure has been repeated by later historians but is obviously too high, since little more than 4,000 infantry in total fought in this campaign. More reliable documents suggest far fewer skiers: in March 1609, for instance, Boije is again mentioned in Russia, scouting with 150 ski-troops from South-East Finland.

There is no evidence for ski-troops in the Prussian or German campaigns; but they continued, long after Gustavus's death, to harass the Russian and Lithuanian cavalry armies on Sweden's 'Eastern front'.

B1: Finnish musketeer

Several Finnish infantry regiments came to Germany with Gustavus, but most were deployed in Latvia, Estonia and along the Russian border. This Finn, based on a German engraving, has dress of Western military type. The coat is probably a 'casack'. Fur caps or similar headgear must have been worn on a large scale by Gustavus's infantry, since there is little evidence for large issues of the broad-brimmed felt hats usually linked with this period. In any case, in battle all infantry were expected to wear helmets. This snaplock musket (LRK 4916) has a butt which resembles the simple early Dutch butt on the engraving.

The skis are based on a crude sketch and description by Johann of Nassau of the strange 'shoes' he observed on Finnish ski-troops: '8 foot long and one hand wide, and made of thin wood... I have seen them several times in Livonia used against the Poles to make strong raids at night on their camp... in the middle is a leather band in which one puts the foot... if there is something of a hill, they attach fur to the left "shoe" one hand wide and made from reindeer skin so that one can get a grip.' At this period a single long ski-pole was more common than a pair. The plate at the base of the pole was often simply a flat disc of wood.

A Lapp wearing unmatched skis. The smaller ski on one foot is known in ski jargon as an 'Andur' or 'Andor', and is lined on the underside with fur to give a better grip on the snow and to prevent backsliding when going uphill. For downhill stretches the skier glided on the broader unlined ski on his other foot. Like most of his contemporaries, he uses only a single long ski-pole. The crossbow remained in use in remoter parts of Scandinavia mostly for hunting. From Johannes Schefferus, Lapponia *(Frankfurt, 1673).*

B2: Lapp, reindeer and sledge

Three companies of Lapps along with reindeers and sledges arrived in Stettin in November 1631, according to one German broadsheet. The report may have just been propaganda, since some Imperialists, at least, were convinced that Gustavus's successes were due to the Lapps in his army 'who cast a spell upon their enemies and prevented them from offering any resistance'.

Thanks to several early travellers, 17th-century Lapp dress is fairly well documented; it was made largely from reindeer hide. The bow here is based on an early Swedish Lapp example at Örbyhus Castle. It is of composite construction covered in birch bark, and very similar to those described by 17th-century travellers. Though already obsolete, bows are occasionally recorded in Gustavus's army. Walter Harte (writing in 1759) mentions as many as 3,000 archers in Swedish service in 1628, but it is not clear who they were. They could not have all been Scots or Irishmen, as the only British regiment to arrive in 1627–28 was Ramsay's, numbering 1,200 men, and it was immediately issued with pikes and muskets. It is more likely that they were newly arrived Finns awaiting re-arming: Finnish 'bowshooters' are men-

tioned in a letter dated April 1627 as being clothed for service away from home.

C: Storming the breach—British mercenaries, 1631

So much has been written about the Scots in Swedish service that the English and Irish have been almost completely overlooked (the Welsh at this time were normally classified as English). The English alone supplied seven regiments between 1624 and 1632. The Irish too had a long tradition as mercenaries, but they were distrusted by Gustavus because of their religion, and served mostly with Catholic powers; even so, several thousand Irish fought in nominally 'Scottish' regiments. In fact, many Englishmen also found their way into 'Scottish' regiments: mercenary colonels were entitled to levy men from any part of the British Isles and certainly did so. For example, James Ramsay's 'Scottish' regiment in 1629 had three English companies, eight Scottish companies (one of which was partly Irish), and one mixed Scottish/English company.

C1: Pikeman, Mackay's/Monro's Scottish Regiment

Romantics would like to believe that Mackay's regiment fought in tartan. In fact, documents in the Danish *Rigsarkivet* record that they received coloured uniforms very soon after their first muster in 1626. When they transferred to Swedish service, 800 of Mackay's men were issued with cloth for uniforms (Royal Wardrobe accounts 1630, item 59). Each man received 8 ells (4.8 metres) of cheap 'Scottish kersey' cloth: twice as much as the normal allowance for a small jacket and breeches. The cloth could have been doubled to give it sufficient thickness, or the excess used for a small cloak or perhaps a casack. The colour of this Scottish kersey is not recorded; in other Swedish documents it appears only in grey or blue, but its low price suggests the same undyed 'hodden grey' cloth common in Scotland. Further evidence for grey comes in June 1631, when a handful of officers of Mackay's regiment were issued grey kersey cloth in Stettin (Royal Wardrobe accounts 1631, item 81).

C2: English musketeer, Hamilton's Army

When it arrived at Stettin in August 1631 the

Marquis of Hamilton's 'English Army', an expeditionary force financed privately by the Stuart royal family, numbered 6,000 men. It was quickly decimated by disease and desertion. The remnants—less than 400 men—did, however, survive long enough to fight at Lützen as part of Lodovick Leslie's (ex-John Hamilton's) Scottish regiment.

There is some evidence for uniforms among Hamilton's troops. In November 1631 the colonels of two of the Marquis's English regiments, James Hamilton and James Ramsay, obtained the following from a merchant in Brandenburg: '500 suits of clothes for soldiers, 500 pair of shoes, 390 pair of stockings, 260 Monmouth caps'. They were required to be 'all according to the patrune [pattern] which we have some' (Scot. Record Office, GD 406/1, 234). A good comparison is the 1627 Privy Council contract apparently for the La Rochelle expedition, ordering '6,000 suits for land soldiers, viz: casacks, hose, cloath[?], shoes, stockings, shirts, [neck]bands and Monmouth caps'. Clearly Monmouth caps were more popular than is usually thought.

C3: Irish Musketeer, Alexander Hamilton's Scottish Regiment

The dress of this Gaelic soldier from Köler's famous Stettin print has many features that can be compared with Irish mainland sources. Köler's jacket, with the peculiar pleated skirt, may be a reflection of actual Irish fashion—similar jackets have been found in Irish bogs (M. Dunlevy, Dress in Ireland (London, 1989)). The felted wool blue bonnet and checked trews are not unique to Scotland; they are found also in Ireland. There is good evidence for the recutting of local Irish cloth (possibly checked) into European style garments such as breeches for service overseas. The Irish mercenaries recruited in 1609 by Spens for Sweden were to be given clothing 'as may cover their nakedness, and only take away the mark of their miserable and barbarous condition'. The clothing was to be 'made of English fashion, but of country [i.e. Irish] stuff, which … is cheap; it being only to serve them at sea, for upon arrival in Sweden they are to receive new apparel and be furnished with arms' (CSP, Ireland, 3 Aug., 1609).

C4: Irish/Highland 'redshanks' recruit

In most cases colonels did not even bother with clothing recruits before shipping them; this Gael still wears his everyday plaid. The export of weapons was forbidden by British law, and eyewitnesses remarked that newly levied mercenaries left Britain and Ireland unarmed except for a few knives and bows carried as personal possessions. Swedish generals often complained of the 'nakedness' of the British recruits, and the need to get them properly clothed even months after they had landed. In Danish service the Scots were often referred to as 'redshanks' (as they were at home) from the ruddy colour of their bare legs. As German cloth supplies grew shorter it became increasingly rare for new arrivals to receive uniforms, so on occasion Highlanders and Irishmen must indeed have gone into action in plaid. But it must be stressed that this was not out of clan or national Gaelic pride in the tartan, but grim economic reality.

D: Flags of the coloured infantry regiments

The colour names of the colour regiments derive from their flags; their origins seem to be connected with the introduction in the 1620s of flags of a single colour.

Until 1620, huge 3 or 4 metre wide flags were used in Sweden. To keep weight down they were made from a very thin silk called kartek. In 1621 the Swedes adopted the smaller 150-man company, and along with this smaller flags that were also Dutch in origin. Weight was no longer such a problem, and so a stronger silk, taffeta, could be used. This was sold in much wider breadths than earlier silks: about 100 cm compared with 33 cm. Pre-1620 flags typically had alternate narrow stripes of at least two different colours; but with the new taffeta flags from 1621 onwards it was less effort to sew a flag of one single colour. After 1627 the amount of taffeta issued for a flag was fixed at 7 ells (4.2 m); allowing for a strip

Shoes recovered from the warship Wasa which sank in Stockholm harbour on its maiden voyage in 1628. The flat-soled variety are probably for ordinary sailors or soldiers (W 19289); the ones with heels perhaps for officers (W8071). (With thanks to Sven Bengtsson of the Sjöhistoriska Museum)

attached to the staff, this made a flag 2 metres (6 ft. 6 in.) square. The similarity of the flags of the Blue, Red and Green Regiments suggests that they were made up in this new pattern at roughly the same time between 1627–28. Reconstructions here are based on Möhner's watercolours of the flags of the Swedish forces occupying Augsburg (1632–35).

D1: The Green Regiment
No specific references to green uniforms for the Green Regiment have yet been found. After describing how the regiment was cajoled into Swedish service, Hoppe (p. 188) explains exactly the origin of its colour name. Gustavus 'ordered *green flags* to be made up for them and [putting them] among the 3 German regiments called the Red, Blue and Yellow, named this one "The Green Regiment" '. Surviving tailor's accounts (transcripts in the Swedish Trophy Collection archive made by Arné Danielsson) confirm that Klitzing, the regiment's new colonel, received taffeta for eight new flags in July 1627. One eighth of the silk was white, which may have been for a separate colonel's 'lifestandard', or (more probably) for devices sewn into the green field.

D2: The Red Regiment
In July 1627 the Red Regiment was issued with eight new crimson taffeta flags, and in November 1628 one flag of red double taffeta. At the bridge at Wittenberg on 13 September 1631 one unit of the Swedish army, almost certainly the Red Regiment, was seen with 7 red, 1 white, and 4 mixed red/white colours. The only references to red uniform come when Hoppe mentions 'German redcoats' under the Red Regiment's Col. Ehrenreiter in June 1628; and 'redcoats' again in August 1630, under Hogendorf, the new colonel.

D3: The Blue Regiment, 1632
It is fairly certain that the Blue Regiment wore blue uniforms. Hoppe writes of Col. Teuffel's and Col. Noth's 'bluecoats' in Prussia, both at dates when they commanded the Blue Regiment; in January 1628 he even names the captains of three companies of 'bluecoats', and all of them definitely held posts in the Blue Regiment. Imperialist descriptions make it fairly clear that the regiment wore blue at Breitenfeld and Lützen.

The peculiar idea that Lapps rode on the backs of reindeer seems to go back to illustrations on the first map of Scandinavia, the Carta marina of 1539 by Olaus Magnus, and his Historia de gentibus septentrionalibus—History of the Northern Peoples— of 1555, shown here. These images are about as reliable as the '200 foot long worms' he shows engulfing ships elsewhere. Less suspect sources show Lapps seated in reindeer-drawn sledges. The strange shoe-like skis are also not to be relied on.

The Swedish historians Zeeh and Nordström think these flags belong to a native Swedish unit, the 'New Blue' Regiment, rather than the mercenary Blue Regiment. They assume that flag D4 is the only flag shown by Möhner of the mercenary Blue Regiment. However, they overlook the fact that there are too many flags for the normal eight-company native Swedish regiment, whereas the mercenary Blue Regiment in 1632 had 12 companies.

Six months after Möhner saw these flags in Augsburg in April 1632, the Blue Regiment lost most of them at Lützen. Deodati noted that they were so tattered by then that little more than empty staffs remained, and it was not thought worthwhile to send them as trophies to the Emperor.

D4: The 'Old Blue' Regiment, c.1633–35
The mercenary Blue Regiment was brought back up to strength in 1633, and from about this time was

Wild men of the multinational Swedish Army: here an Irishman, a Lapp and a Finn. The Finn's overgarment is slightly puzzling, and is probably a casack rather than a buffcoat. From a 1631 German broadsheet.

called the 'Old Blue' Regiment; it must have been issued with new colours, of which this is one. The colonel of the regiment, Winckel, became governor of Augsburg until 1635 while he recovered from wounds received at Lützen. This gave Möhner, who lived in Augsburg, plenty of opportunity to paint this flag in detail: the remaining companies of the regiment were with the field army.

D5: The Yellow Regiment

Gustavus's first guard regiments had flags made in his personal livery colours, yellow and black. Both the old *Hovregiment* (in 1621 and 1622) and the new *Hovregiment* (in May 1624) received flags with yellow and black stripes.

In about 1625 or 26 the *Hovregiment* began to be called the 'Yellow Regiment'. The first record (accounts are incomplete) of all-yellow flags comes in July 1627, when two companies (Winckel's and Koskull's) received the new 2 metre square flags. In May 1630 two further companies (Heussler's and Lichnofsky's) were issued by the Royal Wardrobe with similar yellow flags. An observer who watched the Swedish army cross the bridge at Wittenberg on 13 September 1631 seems to have thought the Yellow Regiment's flags were white. Möhner's watercolours do indeed show them as a very pale yellow colour.

According to Watts, the Yellow Regiment lost seven flags at Lützen (see Plate F). In 1633 the regiment passed to Maj.-Gen. Lars Kagg (Möhner calls it 'General-Major Kage Yellow Leib Regiment'). The flags shown by Möhner may have been replacements. Khevenhüller also records yellow flags for Kagg's regiment at Regensburg in July 1634.

E: Infantry colours: other regiments

Army accounts show that flags of Scottish mercenary regiments were in at least 50% of cases made from blue and white cloth in the correct proportions to make the Scottish flag. In 1635 Ogier saw a Scottish regiment in Prussia 'with huge red flags in the corner of which there is a white cross of St. Andrew and blue field'. English regiments probably also used this English Civil War type of system.

The tattered state of many flags on Möhner's watercolours is typical for Gustavus's veteran regiments over 1630–32; new flags were rarely issued unless a regiment had suffered such drastic casualties that it had to be completely reformed.

E1: Vitzthum's (Orange) Regiment

Möhner's watercolours show the tattered remains of four orange-red flags of 'Obrist Viztumb Regiment'. All are similar. There were several Colonel Vitzthums in Swedish service in 1632, but the state of the flags suggests that Johann Vitzthum von Eckstädt's 'Orange' Regiment raised in 1630 is the only likely candidate. The laurel wreath device is similar to wreaths on Polish flags of the period, so the flag may have been painted in Polish Prussia where the regiment was stationed in 1630.

E2: Wildenstein's (Black) Regiment

Wildenstein's (ex-Hall's) was one of the three or four Black Regiments raised in 1629–30. Wildenstein was killed at Lützen. Aside from Möhner's watercolours, the only direct evidence that the various black regiments had black flags comes in July 1634, when Khevenhüller noted that Count Thurn's (ex-Sperreuter's) regiment carried them at Regensburg. Work by Arné Danielsson on flags in the Swedish Trophy Collection shows that black silk deteriorates more quickly than any other colour. The white flag probably belongs to the colonel's company.

The colour of the various black regiments' uniforms is not recorded. Black cloth was more expensive than other colours, since it had to be dyed in several dyestuffs in turn, and tended to turn green if this was not done carefully. Wallhausen in 1621 specifically discouraged black uniforms on grounds of cost. However, in May 1630 the Royal Wardrobe issued some rather expensive 'coloured broadcloth' to Falkenberg's and Sperreuter's (black) regiments, and this may well have been black.

E3: Wilhelm Bürt's old White Regiment, 1632
The three complete flags show the King's initials (G)ustavus (A)dolphus (R)ex (S)ueciae, together with state and dynastic emblems including the Vasa wheatsheaf. A further seven tattered colours are shown, suggesting a fairly old regiment. The fact that there are ten flags in all and not eight makes identification with Bürt's (ex-Damitz's) 12-company strong White Regiment fairly certain.

E4: Mitschefall's Regiment
Regiments without colour names easily outnumbered ones that had them. Such regiments often had flags with two colours, each company having a slightly different and unique pattern.

Wilhelm Kaspar Mitschefall was commissioned to raise a regiment of 12 companies in August 1629; most of his men, like their colonel, were previously in Danish service. He was executed in September 1632 for unnecessarily surrendering the fortress of Rain,

and his regiment was amalgamated with Bürt's (white) regiment to form Knyphausen's new regiment.

E5: Houwald's Regiment
Christof von Houwald's foot regiment was levied in early 1632, mostly in the Frankfurt-am-Main area. The (until then) unspoilt nature of this wealthy region allowed the raising of 16 companies. Only one flag is shown by Möhner with a 'G' in the canton; the other companies each bore a different letter, so that when all the flags were arranged in sequence they spelt out an abbreviation of 'GUSTAVUS ADOLPHUS REX SUECORUM'. (This flag is incorrectly identified in Wise and Rosignoli's *Military Flags of the World*, 1977).

E6: Schlammersdorf's Regiment
See black and white illustration for description.

E7: Kaspar Ermes' Finnish Regiment
Lt. Col. Kaspar Ermes originally commanded half of Klas Hastfehr's Finnish (Savolax) regiment. He became a colonel in 1634, possibly of his old regiment, and was stationed in Augsburg. Unfortunately, Ermes' flags are the only definite example of native Swedish/Finnish infantry flags to survive among the Möhner paintings. The tailor's accounts give a little further information. In the early 1620s

'In such garments go the 800, in Stettin arrived, Irishmen or Irren' states the caption to this famous print by the Nuremberger Georg Köler. These tartan-clad soldiers are incorrectly described in most modern histories as Highlanders of Mackay's regiment. They can now confidently be identified with Alexander Hamilton's regiment of Scots and Irish, which landed near Stettin in August 1631 as part of the Marquis of Hamilton's British expedition. They may in fact have been true Irishmen: Alexander Hamilton's 1632 muster rolls unmistakably Irish names like Huigh O'Doherty and Farrel O'Galihor.

In folchem Habit Gehen die 800 In Stettin angekommen Irrlander oder Irren.

many regiments were issued with cloth of the same colours as the provincial arms; by the late 1620s this was less common. In a few cases at least flags seem to have been painted with provincial arms. Flags of more than one colour are common, for example Hoppe notes that Col. Thomas Muschamp's [Småland] infantry in 1628 had 'new yellow flags with a red cross therein'.

F: The Old Guard: The Yellow Regiment at Lützen, 1632

On 16 November 1632 Gustavus was killed leading his cavalry at Lützen. The fate of his infantry was less widely publicised: in an attack on the Imperialist centre against men who had begun to copy Swedish tactics, the Yellow and the Blue Regiments and the Swedish brigade are reported to have suffered up to 75% casualties. Their defeat is recorded by Watts: 'the chief spoyle light upon the two middlemost Brigades of Foote… [The Yellow and the Blue]… the flower of the Army: old souldiers of 7 or 8 yeeres service, (the most of them) and whom the King had there placed, for that he most relied on them… Their bodies now covered the same ground which living they had defended. These were old beaten [i.e. seasoned] souldiers, indeed, but it was so long since they had been last beaten, that they had by this time forgotten how to runne away.'

An Italian officer, Deodati, also witnessed their ruin from the Imperialist lines: 'A great body with yellow casacks came up resolutely in formation and with pikes covering up their musketeers. When attacked by our infantry it was completely overthrown, and it was a wonder to see in a moment the body reduced to a hill of corpses. The blue casacks [either the Blue Regiment or the Swedish brigade] had no better luck…'

F1 & F2: Musketeer and Pikeman, Yellow Regiment

The Yellow Regiment appears to have worn yellow coats at least since January 1627, when Hoppe first refers to Col. Teuffel's 'squadron of Yellowcoats'. (New uniforms of unspecified colour were issued to the regiment in Elbing late in 1626.) 'German Yellowcoats'—almost certainly the Yellow Regiment—are mentioned again by Hoppe in August 1629. Yellow 'casacche' are mentioned at Breitenfeld by Gualdo Priorato and again by Deodati at Lützen; in both cases these must refer to the Yellow Regiment. On 27 October 1632 new clothing (of unspecified type and colour) was ready for the regiment in Nuremberg, and this may have reached it in time for the battle of Lützen.

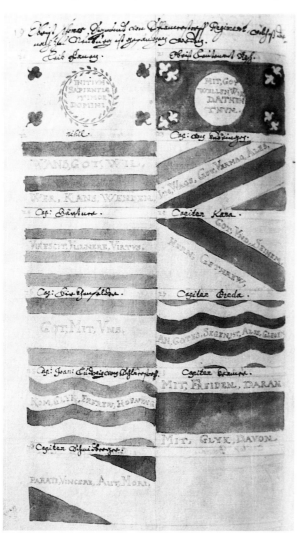

These little-known watercolour paintings in a manuscript by Reginbaldus Möhner contain details of the flags of a small part of Gustavus's army; they date from the Swedish occupation of Augsburg from 1632 to 1635. Each company at this period had its own flag, and by 1631 several ingenious systems had appeared to differentiate between the companies of a regiment, while maintaining a regimental theme, as here on the green and white flags of Thomas Sigmund von Schlammersdorf's first mercenary regiment. This unit of 11 companies was raised in 1631, and stationed in Augsburg for much of its existence; it was captured at Neuburg in 1633 by the Bavarians.

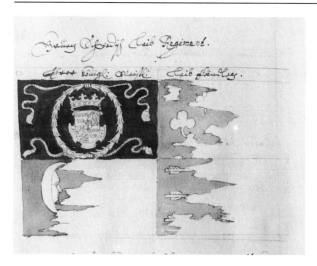

The flag of Gustavus's Lifeguard company (top left), and three tattered colours of the 'Green Swedish Life Regiment'. This first flag (see also Plate F) has been misidentified in most modern works, even though Möhner correctly describes it as 'His Roy[al] Maj[esty]'s Life Standard'. It is shown here among the Green Regiment's flags because its commander, Pfuel, was promoted to the colonelcy of the Green Regiment in place of Hepburn early in 1632. It later returned to its customary place alongside the Yellow Regiment.

Rather than attempt a reconstruction of casacks from the contradictory source material, we here base the coats of the Yellow Regiment on the many pictures by Merian of Frankfurt, who illustrated the great history of the Thirty Years' War *Theatrum Europaeum*, published first in the late 1630s. Though not entirely reliable as a uniform source, Merian illustrates a trend already apparent by 1630 for breeches to get tighter and jackets to get longer. In 1627, for example, Gustavus ordered a 'large number' of 'Hungarian jackets [*jackor*], which should reach down to the middle of the breeches, and then breeches narrow below the knee'.

F3: 'Commanded' musketeer, Yellow Regiment
The surplus musketeers not needed in the main brigade formation were often 'out-commanded' or detached for other duties; among these was service as 'a forlorn hope' in front of the main brigades. Some historians have suggested that they used light muskets without rests. Though there is evidence for such muskets by 1632, it cannot be proved that they were issued specifically to commanded musketeers. They would certainly have been well-suited, since commanded men were often given horses for mounted

duties; by 1633 one company of the Yellow Regiment was permanently equipped with horses and re-classed as dragoons.

The dress of commanded men would not have differed significantly from the rest of the regiment, though some improvisation may have taken place to adapt them to what was essentially a light infantry rôle. Monmouth caps seem to be shown on a print of Swedish troops in Augsburg in 1632, and could be appropriate.

F4: Musketeer, King's Lifeguard company
The King's Lifeguard was an independent company not part of a regiment which acted as Gustavus's personal bodyguard. It was usually brigaded with the Yellow Regiment. The Lifeguard's clothing is known in some detail because it was issued almost annually by the Royal Wardrobe. On 26 January 1632, in Frankfurt-am-Main, the 72 musketeers of the Lifeguard each received clothing made from 12 ells of grey broadcloth with 240 small thread buttons, and grey hats (Royal Wardrobe Accounts 1632, item 29).

F5: Ensign, King's Lifeguard company
Instead of pikemen, the Lifeguard had 65 *Upwarter* ('attendants') who carried partisans, at least on ceremonial duty. They were trusted veterans, with a higher proportion of officers than normal: eight of the 35 men of the company hospitalised after Lützen held the rank of ensign.

This ensign is dressed in the clothes issued to an *Upwarter* at Frankfurt in January 1632. His striped coat (called a 'kappa' in the accounts) was made from 10 ells of grey French broadcloth, decorated with 26 ells of silver galloon. We reconstruct it from prints that seem to show Lifeguards near Frankfurt in winter 1631–32, and from a similar yellow 'livery coat' with horizontally applied galloon in the *Livrustkammaren*. The casack was originally a garment of this type, and similar coats in yellow may have been worn by the entire Yellow Regiment. The Lifeguard company was one of the only units to be issued with buffcoats, probably because they were expected to accompany Gustavus on horseback. These buffcoats, which were issued only to *Upwater*, were made from elk hide with buck hide sleeves, and cost 12 Rdr. each. Breeches, clearly for winter wear, were also supplied; each pair was made from one large sheepskin.

45

The note in Swedish attached to the sleeve states 'This satin doublet was worn by Count Nils Brahe when he was shot at Lützen'. Brahe was general of the infantry at Lützen, and received a fatal thigh wound during the battle. The doublet is now a faded tan–yellow colour, an interesting coincidence since Brahe was also the colonel of the Yellow Regiment. (Bielke Armoury, Skokloster)

'To tell the truth' wrote Watts in an embarrassed tone, 'the Kings own company which served here [at Lützen] among the Guards, lost their owne Ensigne or Standard Royall too.' Luckily, Möhner made a watercolour sketch of the Lifeguard's flag in April 1632, and the tailor's accounts also survive. In 1625, 1627, 1629, 1631 and 1642 the Royal Wardrobe issued silk for the Lifeguard's flag; when the colour was specified it was always black decorated with gold leaf. The flag carried at Lützen was almost certainly the one issued in Frankfurt on 18 November 1631, consisting of 8 ells of black Naples taffeta, giving dimensions of about 2 m × 2.25 m (Royal Wardrobe accounts 1632, item 4). An elaborate gilded silver finial, claimed to be the 'staffhead of Gustav Adolf's Life Standard', has also survived. It belonged, in 1945, to an Italian Contessa living near Udine (photo: LRK E4696).

F6: Colonel, Yellow Regiment

Count Nils Brahe commanded the Yellow Regiment at Lützen. Gustavus considered him the ablest Swede in the army after his artillery commander Lennart Torstensson. Brahe had studied at Leiden, and progressed rapidly in the army on his return. At only 23 he became colonel of the senior national unit, the Uppland Regiment. In 1631 he took over the Yellow Regiment, and in 1632, at the age of only 28, was made General of the Infantry. He commanded the front four brigades at Lützen and was wounded in the left leg during the battle, dying a fortnight later.

A 1703 inventory of Brahe's family church lists a jacket (see monochrome illustrations) plus a buffcoat (now disappeared) lying on his casket. The suggestion is that both were worn at Lützen, the buffcoat completely covering the jacket. His appearance here is based on a full-length portrait at Gripsholm.

G: Destitution: North Germany and Prussia, 1634/5

Gustavus's death dampened Swedish enthusiasm for the war in Germany: Chancellor Axel Oxenstierna took over control of both state and army, but for him the catastrophic defeat at Nördlingen in 1634 was almost the last straw: 'I will struggle no longer, but drift where the tide will take me...' In 1633 he had

already withdrawn most native Swedish regiments to north Germany, leaving the new German mercenary units to sort out their own problems in southern Germany. Oddly enough, it was the 'safe' northern garrisons that suffered the most: from hunger and disease rather than war. The conditions in Marienberg in Polish Prussia in 1635 particularly appalled the French diplomat Ogier: 'I looked over the camp and shelters of the Swedes, where I saw a true picture of human destitution and folly. I saw the faces of men, and since I did not notice them talking or conversing, I doubted if they really were people at all; so barbarous, dirty, sick were they, and all tattered and barefoot, for the greater part rude peasant youths. And these are the very Swedes, who are forcing many countries from the field and plough to war...'

G1: Swedish peasant recruit

This figure is based on a picture made by Lorenzo Magalotti in Sweden in 1674 (colours are added on this reconstruction). 'Peasant grey' wool was typical for homespun garments like this jacket. The coloured piping was probably influenced by Gustavus's instructions to insert coloured cloth in the seams of military garments to make them more colourful. The clothing is more than passingly similar to that of Polish/Prussian peasants in the 1630s (see Plate D, MAA 184: *Polish Armies 1569–1696 (1)*).

G2: Swedish musketeer, 1633 mourning uniform

In 1633 Gustavus's body was transported north, ready for a state funeral in Stockholm. At Wolgast in north Germany the veteran Swedish infantry accompanying the body received new black uniforms. They numbered only 1,648 men in all, in four 'regiments' (most native Swedish regiments in Germany were heavily amalgamated by this time so that their provincial identities are unclear). Each uniform was made from six ells of black 'piuk' cloth lined with black material called 'boy', together with a black hat (Royal Wardrobe accounts, June/July 1633). Some regiments also received black flags. Because of cloth shortages these black uniforms may have been worn long after the funeral ceremony in 1634.

G3: Veteran wearing Hongreline

Few pictures survive of Gustavus's soldiers in winter clothing. We might expect a strong Eastern influence from neighbouring Russia and Poland, but when winter garments are mentioned they are usually called 'Lappish'. The winter clothing here is, however, clearly east European in origin. It is based on a Swede in a 1640s battle painting by Snayers in the Heeresgeschichtliches Museum, Vienna.

This type of fur coat was sometimes called a *Hongreline* (a term derived from the word 'Hungary'). The fur hat and long tight trousers were also copied from Croat, Polish and Hungarian light cavalry that served the Imperialists. These warm and practical garments became increasingly popular in the later stages of the Thirty Years' War, and must have helped to inspire the long military jackets that began to appear in Western military fashion by the 1650s.

Farbtafeln

A Norrland

A1 Gleichfarbige Jacke und Hose waren noch keine Uniform, die Einheiten identifizierten; der Stoff wurde jedoch als Massenware gekauft und in Einzelfarben ausgegeben. Der Morion ist norddeutsch; die Halsberge war wahrscheinlich ein Rangabzeichen. Die Waffe ist ein leichter, altmodischer Caliver. **A2** Dies wurde – wie das meiste auf dieser Aufnahme – wahrscheinlich nach einem Portrait von Oberst Duwall vom Norrland Landsregiment rekonstruiert. **A3** Offiziere ließen den ihnen zugeteilten Stoff privat schneidern. Weiße Federn scheinen bei diesem Regiment allgemein üblich gewesen zu sein; die Farben der Schärpen variierten je nach Schwadron. Er trägt eine holländische Partisan guter Qualität. **A4** Rekonstruktion nach verschiedenen Quellen, und zeitgenössische holländische und deutsche Stücke. **A5** Die dekorativere Kleidung zeigt wahrscheinlich das 'Oberst-Schwadron' an. Die 'Saufeder-Stange' entspricht Augenzeugenberichten.

B1 Nach einer deutschen Radierung. Westliche Kleidung mit Pelzmütze, die in der ganzen Armee von Gustav üblich war; der Mantel dürfte ein 'Casack' sein. Die Schnappschloß-Muskete ist in holländischem Stil. Johann von Nassau hat die Skier beschrieben; ein einziger Skistock wurde verwendet. **B2** Bei Stettin sollen 1631 drei Kompanien gewesen sein, und Reisende hinterließen Beschreibungen der Lappen-Kostüme, die hauptsächlich aus Rentierfellen angefertigt wurden. Ein Bogen hat überlebt; es gab Bogenschützen in Gustavs Armee, allerdings nur in geringer Anzahl.

C1 Schwedische Stoffe, wahrscheinlich in stumpfem Grau oder Blau, wurden diesen schottischen Truppen zur Anfertigung von Uniformen ausgeliefert. **C2** Nur etwa 400 Mann von 6.000 überlebten, um bei Lützen zu kämpfen – Krankheit und Fahnenflucht hatten Opfer gefordert. Aus Kontobüchern der zeit geht hervor, daß in Brandenburg gekaufte Uniformstoffe erhalten wurden, einschließlich von 'Monmouth-Mützen'. **C3** Irisch-gälischer Soldat nach dem berühmten Stettindruck von Köler, bestätigt durch zeitgenössische irische Quellen. **C4** Rekruten trafen oft in mangelhafter Kleidung und Bewaffnung ein, und als die deutschen Lieferungen seltener wurden, dürften viele Rekruten immer noch in den ärmlichsten eingeborenen Trachten in den Kampf gezogen sein.

D Die Farbbezeichnungen der Regimenter wurden von ihren Fahnen abgeleitet – oft in Einzelfarben und den späte 20.er Jahren des 17.Jahrhunderts, etwa 2 m lang und aus Taffeta hergestellt. **D1** Diese Einheit (für deren angeblich grüne Uniformen es keine Beweise gibt), erhilet im Juli 1627 grünen Stoff für acht Fahnen, zusammen mit etwas weißem Stoff, wahrscheinlich für Muster auf den Fahnen – möglicherweise eine weiße 'Obristen-Lebensflagge'. **D2** 1631 dürfte das die Einheit gewesen sein, die sieben rote, eine weiße und vier rotweiße Fahnen gehabt haben soll. Es gibt ganz wenige Hinweise auf rote Uniformen. **D3** Sie trugen bei Breitenfeld und Lützen wahrscheinlich blaue Uniformen; bei Lützen verlor diese deutsche Söldnertruppe die meisten ihrer Fahnen, die zu diesem Zeitpunkt bereits recht zerfetzt waren. **D4** Dem neugebildeten blauen Regiment wurden neue Fahnen verliehen; das Regiment wurde seit 1633 das 'alte blaue' genannt. **D5** Gustavs Garderegimenter trugen Anfang der 20er Jahre des 17.Jahrhunderts gelb- und schwarzgestreifte Fahnen; reine gelbe wurden 1627 ausgegeben; sieben davon gingen bei Lützen verloren. Die Farbe war offenbar sehr blaß.

E1 Viele schwedische Fahnen waren sehr zerfetzt; sie wurden selten ausgewechselt – erst wenn ein fast vernichtetes Regiment neu geformt wurde. **E2** Dies war eines von drei oder vier 'schwarzen' Regimentern; die weiße Fahne ist wohl die der Kompanie des Obristen. Schwarze Uniformen waren besonders kostspielig, dürften aber doch vorhanden gewesen sein. **E3** Die kompletten Fahnen zeigen die königlichen Initialen 'G A' sowie 'RS' für 'Rex Sueciae', mit verschiedenen Emblemen, darunter die Weizengarbe der Wasa-Dynastie. **E4** Regimenter ohne Farbbezeichnungen waren die große Mehrheit; sie hatten häufig zweifarbige Fahnen, nach Kompanien unterschiedlich. **E5** Eine große Einheit, aufgestellt in dem damals noch nicht verwüsteten Gebiet von Frankfurt; ihre 16 Kompanien, deren Fahnen jeweils einin verschiedenen Buchstaben im Feld zeigten, so daß sie bei einer Aufstellung in richtiger Reihenfolge eine Abkürzung des Namens und Titel von Gustav Adolf ergaben. **E6** Siehe Bildtext zur Schwarzweiß-Abbildung. **E7** Das einzige definitive Beispiel für die Fahnen einer schwedische-finnischen Einheit, das unter den Bildern von Möhner überlebt hat.

F1,2 Diese deutschen Söldner trugen gelbe 'Casacks', die wenigstens aus dem Jahre 1627 stammten; die Quellen sind jedoch widersprüchlich, und diese Rekonstruktionen beruhen auf den langen ungarischen Jacken, die Merian 1630 zeigte, zusammen mit Breeches. **F3** In der Rolle leichter Infanterie, manchmal auch beritten, ist dieser Musketier mit einer Monmouth-Mütze rekonstruiert, und er benutzt eine der leichteren Musketen ohne Stütze. **F4** Die unabhängige Leibgarde-Kompanie hat eine Tracht, die detailliert in manchen Bekleidungsaufzeichnungen festgehalten ist. **F5** Partisanen wurden anstelle von Piken verwendet; diese Einheit hatte einen großen Prozentsatz an Offizieren und viele erfahrene Veteranen. Seine Tracht wurde in Frankfurt 1632 aufgezeichnet – als Kappa-Mantel, grau mit silbernen Streifen; andere Quellen haben dieser Rekonstruktion geholfen. Den Ledermantel gab es nur in dieser Einheit. **F6** Beruhend auf einem Portrait des Obersten Nils Brahe, tödlich verwundet bei Lützen, sowie auf Familiendokumenten.

G Die Armee litt zu jener Zeit unter Hunger, Krankheit und Mangel. **G1** Schwedische Bauerntracht in Grau; Gustav befahl, die Tracht durch Paspels mit farbigen Bändern zu beleben. **G2** Neue schwarze Uniformen und Fahnen wurden an die 1.648 Mann ausgegeben, die die Leiche Gustavs heimwärts eskortierten. **G3** Winterkleidung, beruhend auf einem Gemälde von Snayers aus dem Jahre 1640, jetzt in Wien; der Mantel trug die Bezeichnung Hongrecline, was sich auf Ungarn bezog; Mütze und Hose sind auch polnisch/kroatisch/ungarischer Art, was spät im Dreißigjährigen Krieg sehr beliebt war.

Notes sur les planches en couleur

A Norrland Landsregiment.

A1 Les vestes et pantalons de couleur identique n'étaient pas encore des uniformes identifiant les unités; le drap était acheté et distribué par lot de même couleur cependant. Le style du morion provient de l'Allemagne du Nord; le hausse-col est probablement la marque de son grade. Il est armé d'un caliver léger, plutôt suranné. **A2** C'est une reconstitution, comme la plupart de cette gravure, d'après un portrait de Colonel Duwall du Norrland Landsregiment. **A3** Les officiers se faisaient tailler leur habit dans le privé avec le tissu qui leur était distribué. Il semble que les plumes blanches étaient courantes pour l'ensemble de ce régiment; les couleurs de la ceinture d'étoffe variaient selon l'escadron. Il a un partisan hollandais de bonne qualité. **A4** Une reconstitution d'après des sources variées, et des pièces d'époque hollandaises et allemandes. **A5** La tenue plus ornée indique probablement qu'il s'agit de l'escadron du colonel'. Le pieu à 'plume de porc' est tiré de récits de témoins oculaires.

B1 D'après une gravure allemande. Tenue occidentale, avec le bonnet de fourrure qui devait être courant dans toute l'armée de Gustave II Adolphe; le manteau est probablement un 'casack'. Le mousquet est à ressort est de style hollandais. Johann de Nassau a décrit les skis; on utilisait alors un seul bâton. **B2** Trois compagnies auraient été à Stettin en 1631; et des voyageurs laissèrent des descriptions du costume de Lapp, fait en grande partie de peau de renne. On a conservé un arc composite; les archers étaient bien représentés dans l'armée de Gustave II Adolphe, quoiqu'en petits nombres.

C1 Une étoffe suédoise, probablement de la grosse toile grise ou bleue, avait été distribuée à ces troupes écossaises pour s'en faire des costumes. **C2** Seuls quelque 400 hommes sur les 6000 survécurent suffisamment de temps pour se battre à Lützen; les autres succombèrent à la maladie ou désertèrent. On sait d'après des livres de compte qu'ils reçurent des vêtements d'uniforme achetés à Brandebourg, y compris des 'bonnets Monmouth'. **C3** Soldat gaélique irlandais, d'après la célèbre édition de Stettin par Köler, qui correspond aux sources irlandaises de cette époque. **C4** Les recrues arrivaient souvent pauvrement pourvues en vêtements et armes, et au fur et à mesure que les approvisionnements allemands se firent plus rares, elles semblent avoir dû se rendre au combat toujours vêtues de leur costume natif le plus basique.

D Les 'noms de couleur' des régiments étaient dérivés de leurs drapeaux, tous d'une seule couleur, dès la fin des années 1620, de 2m environ et faits en taffetas. **D1** Cette unité (dont on a aucun témoignage sur les uniformes verts) reçut l'étoffe verte pour huit drapeaux en juillet 1627, avec un peu d'étoffe blanche, certainement pour les emblèmes, peut-être pour une bannière de colonel. **D2** En 1631 l'unité pourrait être celle décrite comme ayant sept drapeaux rouges, un blanc et quatre rouge et blanc. Il n'y a que de très rares allusions à des uniformes rouges. **D3** Ils portaient probablement des uniformes bleus à Breitenfeld et Lützen; cette unité de mercenaires allemands perdit presque tous ses drapeaux à cette dernière bataille, ceux-ci étaient alors en lambeaux. **D4** De nouveaux drapeaux furent distribués au Régiment Bleu reconstitué, qui fut nommé l'"Ancien Bleu" à partir de 1633. **D5** Les régiments de la garde de Gustave II Adolphe utilisèrent des drapeaux à raies jaunes et noires au début des années 1620; des drapeaux entièrement jaunes commencèrent à être distribués en 1627; sept furent perdus à Lützen. La couleur était apparemment très pâle.

E1 De nombreux drapeaux suédois étaient en loques, étant rarement remplacés sauf lorsqu'un régiment était reformé après avoir été quasiment annihilé. **E2** C'était l'un des trois ou quatre régiments 'Noirs'; la bannière blanche est probablement celle de la compagnie du colonel. Les uniformes noirs étaient particulièrement chers, mais peut-être pas inexistants. **E3** Les bannières complètes portent les initiales du roi 'G A' et 'RS' pour 'Rex Sueciae', avec plusieurs emblèmes y compris la gerbe de blé de Vasa. **E4** Les régiments sans noms de couleurs étaient la grande majorité. Ils avaient souvent des bannières à deux couleurs selon les compagnies. **E5** Une grande unité recrutée dans la région de Francfort alors épargnée, ses seize compagnies avaient chacune une lettre différente dans le canton pour épeler lors de leur appel dans l'ordre le nom et le titre de Gustave II Adolphe. **E6** Voir la légende de l'illustration en noir et blanc. **E7** Le seul exemple défini des bannières d'une unité native suédoise/finlandaise qui ait subsisté parmi les tableaux de Möhner.

F1,F2 Ces mercenaires allemands portèrent des 'casacks' jaunes à partir de 1627 au moins; mais les sources sont contradictoires, et ces reconstitutions sont basées sur les longues vestes 'hongroises' représentées par Merian en 1630, avec des culottes plus serrées qu'auparavant. **F3** Ce mousquetaire, en détachement dans l'infanterie légère et à cheval quelquefois, est reconstitué avec un bonnet Monmouth, et l'un des mousquets les plus légers qui étaient utilisés sans fourche. **F4** L'habit de la compagnie de la Garde du corps indépendante est enregistré avec un certain détail dans les comptes annuels de la Garde-robe. **F5** On utilisait des partisans au lieu de piques; cette unité avait une proportion élevée d'officiers et de nombreux vétérans pleins d'expérience. Son costume fut enregistré à Francfort, en 1632, comme un manteau kappa de drap gris avec rayures d'argent, d'autres sources aident à le reconstituer. Le pourpoint de buffle était unique à cette unité. **F6** Basé sur le portrait de Colonel Nils Brahe, blessé mortellement à Lützen, et sur des documents familiaux.

G La famine, la maladie et le plus complet dénuement accablaient l'armée à cette période. **G1** Fondamentalement, costume de paysan suédois en gris: Gustave II Adolphe ordonna que les coutures soient avivées par des passements en ruban de couleur. **G2** De nouveaux uniformes et drapeaux noirs furent distribués aux 1648 hommes qui escortèrent le corps de Gustave II Adolphe sur le chemin du retour. **G3** Tenue d'hiver, basée sur un tableau de Snayers, de 1640, maintenant à Vienne; la veste s'appelait une Hongreline, rappelant son origine hongroise, et le bonnet et les pantalons son également de style polonais/croate/hongrois, qui devint de plus en plus en vogue à la fin de la Guerre de 30 Ans.